Digital Shield: A Girl's Ultimate Guide t Safety

Protecting Yourself from Online Threats, Scams & Exploitation

Preface

The internet has revolutionized the way we **connect, learn, and share** our lives with the world. Social media, in particular, has provided young girls with an incredible platform for:

- **Self-expression**

- **Creativity**

- **Communication**

However, with this freedom comes a **darker reality**—one filled with:

- **Cyberbullying**

- **Online predators**

- **Scams**

- **Privacy breaches**

- **Serious dangers like human trafficking**

As technology evolves, so do the tactics of those who seek to exploit others. Today, young girls face threats that previous generations never encountered, including:

- **Fake profiles & identity theft**

- **Deepfake manipulation**

- **Romance scams & social media grooming**

1

While social media platforms claim to have safety measures in place, the responsibility of protection **ultimately falls on the user**. But how can young girls protect themselves if they don't even know what to look out for?

That's why this book was written—to serve as a **digital shield**, empowering girls with the knowledge and tools needed to navigate the online world **safely**. Unlike other books that focus **only** on cyberbullying or mental health, this guide goes **deeper**, uncovering **hidden dangers** such as:

- **Human trafficking recruiters**

- **Financial scams & phishing**

- **Privacy breaches & hacking**

- **Psychological manipulation by online predators**

In *Digital Shield: A Girl's Ultimate Guide to Social Media Safety*, **you will learn:**

✔ How to **spot and avoid** online scams, phishing, and fraud
✔ How to **secure your accounts** from hacking and impersonation
✔ The **red flags** of online grooming, romance scams, and predatory behavior
✔ How traffickers and criminals use social media to **lure victims**
✔ Ways to **build healthy digital habits** and protect your mental health
✔ **Practical self-defense** strategies for online safety

This book is **not about fear**—it's about **empowerment**. The internet should be a **safe place** for everyone. By reading this guide, you are taking an important step toward **protecting yourself** and staying in control of your digital life.

Your safety matters.
Your voice matters.
Your online world should be as secure as your offline one.

Let's make it happen together.

Stay informed. Stay strong. Stay safe.

— Fazal Abubakkar Esaf

Acknowledgement

Writing this book has been a journey of **deep research, learning, and dedication** to the cause of keeping young girls safe in the digital world. It would not have been possible without the **guidance, support, and encouragement** of many individuals and organizations.

First and foremost, I express my **heartfelt gratitude** to all the **brave girls and women** who have shared their personal experiences with online harassment, scams, and cyber threats.

Your **courage in speaking up** has helped shape this book into a powerful resource that can **protect and empower others**.

I extend my sincere appreciation to **cybersecurity experts, social activists, and mental health professionals**, whose insights and expertise have been invaluable in ensuring the **accuracy and relevance** of the content in this book. Your work in **digital safety and awareness** has inspired me greatly.

A special thank you to my **family and friends** for their unwavering support, patience, and belief in this project. Your encouragement kept me motivated throughout the writing process.

To **teachers, parents, and educators** who work tirelessly to protect and guide young minds—I acknowledge your dedication and hope that this book serves as a **valuable tool** in your mission to create a **safer online space**.

Lastly, I am grateful to **every reader** who picks up this book. By **educating yourself and sharing this knowledge**, you are taking a powerful step toward a **safer, more informed digital world**.

Together, we can create a future where **every girl** can explore the internet **fearlessly, securely, and with confidence**.

— *Fazal Abubakkar Esaf*

Introduction

The digital world has become an **inseparable** part of our lives. From staying connected with friends to learning new skills and exploring opportunities, social media offers **endless possibilities**. However, beneath its vibrant surface lies a **darker reality**—one filled with:

- **Cyberbullying**

- **Online predators**

- **Scams**

- **Privacy breaches**

- **Serious dangers like human trafficking**

For young girls, the risks are especially high. Every day, millions of girls worldwide face threats on social media—whether it's through **unwanted messages, blackmail, hacking, or emotional manipulation**. Some are targeted by **online predators** pretending to be friends, while others are tricked into **scams** that steal their money or personal information. The internet is a place of **both opportunity and danger**, and learning how to navigate it safely is more important than ever.

Why This Book Matters

Many girls are **unaware** of the dangers lurking behind the screens. They may not realize that:

- A **friendly stranger online** could have bad intentions.

- A **simple click on a suspicious link** could compromise their privacy.

- Someone could **use their pictures without permission**.

The internet is filled with **hidden traps**, but **knowledge is the key** to avoiding them.

This book is your **guide to staying safe online**. It will help you:

- **Recognize** online threats like cyberbullying, scams, and digital blackmail.

- **Protect** your personal information and avoid hacking or identity theft.

- **Spot** the warning signs of online grooming and romance scams.

- **Understand** how human traffickers use social media to lure victims.

- **Build confidence** in managing your digital life safely.

What You'll Find in This Book

Each chapter is designed to give you the **knowledge and tools** you need to **protect yourself** in the digital space. You'll learn about:

- **Cybersecurity basics**: How to secure your accounts, set strong passwords, and protect your digital identity.

- **Social media dangers**: From catfishing to cyberbullying, understand the risks and how to handle them.

- **Online scams and fraud**: How to avoid fake giveaways, phishing scams, and financial fraud.

- **Predators and trafficking risks**: How criminals use social media to lure and exploit young girls.

- **Mental health in the digital age**: How to maintain self-esteem, avoid social media addiction, and deal with online pressure.

This book is **not just about fear**—it's about **power**. By learning how to protect yourself, you take **control** of your online experience.

A Safe Online Future Starts With You

Social media should be a place for **connection, creativity, and learning—not fear**. By reading this book, you're taking an important step in **protecting yourself and others** from online threats.

So let's begin. Let's build a **stronger, safer, and more informed digital future—together.**

Stay safe. Stay smart. Stay strong.

— *Fazal Abubakkar Esaf*

Index

Bonus Features

Chapter 1: Why Social Media Safety Matters

The Double-Edged Sword of Social Media

Imagine this: You post a fun picture with your best friend, thinking it's just a harmless moment to share. But within minutes, a stranger saves it, shares it elsewhere, or even uses it to create a fake profile. Meanwhile, someone you don't know sends a direct message that seems friendly—until they start asking for personal details.

This is the reality of social media today.

Platforms like Instagram, TikTok, Snapchat, and Facebook have revolutionized the way we **connect, express ourselves, and explore the world**. They allow us to:

Stay in touch with friends and family
Share creative content and personal milestones
Discover opportunities for learning, networking, and self-growth

But alongside these benefits lurk **serious dangers**—especially for young girls.

The Hidden Dangers of Social Media

Many people think online threats only happen to others. The truth? **Anyone can become a target.** The internet is filled with individuals who manipulate trust, curiosity, and inexperience. Here are some of the biggest risks girls face online:

Cyberbullying – Hurtful comments, rumors, and online harassment can lead to anxiety, depression, and even self-harm.
Online Predators – Strangers pretending to be friendly could actually be grooming or exploiting young girls.
Romance Scams – Fake online relationships are used to manipulate girls into sharing money or personal information.
Privacy Breaches – Personal details, photos, and locations can be

stolen or misused if shared carelessly.

Human Trafficking Risks – Traffickers use social media to target and lure victims with false promises of jobs, love, or opportunities.

Social Media Addiction – Spending too much time online can harm mental health, increase insecurity, and damage real-life relationships.

Real-Life Consequences of Unsafe Online Behavior

Ignoring social media safety can lead to **life-changing consequences**.

Take *Maya*, for example. She was a normal 15-year-old who loved posting selfies and chatting with new online friends. One day, she received a message from someone claiming to be a modeling scout. He told her she had "the perfect look" and invited her to a private photoshoot. The promise of fame and success excited her—but luckily, she mentioned it to her older sister, who immediately saw the red flags. The so-called "scout" was actually a trafficker.

Not every girl is as lucky as Maya. Some end up **scammed, blackmailed, harassed, or worse.** A single mistake—trusting the wrong person, clicking on a suspicious link, or oversharing—can **put your safety at risk.**

The good news? **You have the power to protect yourself.**

How This Book Will Empower You

This book is not about **fear**—it's about **power.** You don't need to stop posting, chatting, or making new friends online. Instead, you need to learn how to **spot dangers and respond smartly.**

Here's what you'll gain from reading this book:

✔ **Recognizing & Avoiding Online Threats** – Learn how to identify scams, predators, and fake profiles.
✔ **Protecting Your Personal Data** – Understand privacy settings, secure your accounts, and stop oversharing.
✔ **Making Smart Choices** – Know when to trust someone, when to block, and how to report harmful behavior.
✔ **Helping Others Stay Safe** – Spread awareness and be part of the change for a safer digital world.

Your Digital Safety Is in Your Hands

Think of your social media like your **home.** You wouldn't leave the front door open for strangers to walk in, right? **So why leave your online doors unlocked?**

Your online presence is an extension of your real life—it deserves the same level of security and awareness.

By the time you finish this book, you'll have the tools and confidence to **take control of your digital world.**

Are you ready to **stay safe, stay smart, and stay strong** in the digital age? Let's begin.

Key Takeaways from This Chapter:

Social media is powerful but comes with risks.
Online threats can affect **anyone**, including you.
Cyberbullies, predators, and scammers **manipulate trust** and

personal information.

Being aware and prepared is the **best defense** against online dangers.

Your **digital safety is in your hands**—and knowledge is your strongest weapon.

Social media is meant to be a place for fun, connection, and creativity—but it can also be a **breeding ground for dangers** if you're not careful. From cyberbullying to online predators, identity theft to privacy violations, the risks are **real** and **affect millions of people every day**—especially young girls.

The good news? **Knowledge is power.** The more you understand these threats, the better you can protect yourself.

---

1. Cyberbullying & Online Harassment

Cyberbullying is one of the **most common** social media dangers. Unlike traditional bullying, it happens **24/7, anonymously, and spreads quickly** through social media, messaging apps, and gaming platforms.

Forms of Cyberbullying

Hateful Comments – Insulting, shaming, or making fun of someone's appearance, beliefs, or lifestyle.
Doxxing – Exposing personal information (home address, phone number, school details) without permission.
Threats & Hate Speech – Sending direct threats or using offensive language to intimidate.
Spreading Rumors – Posting lies or gossip to ruin someone's reputation.
Catfishing & Fake Profiles – Pretending to be someone else to deceive, trick, or embarrass a victim.
Body Shaming – Criticizing someone's looks, weight, or personal choices.
Trolling – Deliberately provoking or harassing people online for attention.

Effects of Cyberbullying

Increased **anxiety, stress, and depression**
Damaged **self-esteem** and growing **self-doubt**
Fear of using social media or engaging online
Sleep disturbances and **academic decline**
In severe cases, **self-harm or suicidal thoughts**

How to Protect Yourself from Cyberbullying

Use Privacy Settings – Control who can comment, message, or see your posts.
Ignore & Don't Engage – Responding often gives bullies more power.
Block & Report – Remove harassers and report them to platform moderators.
Take Screenshots – Save evidence in case you need to report to authorities.
Talk to Someone You Trust – Parents, teachers, or counselors can offer support.

---

2. Online Predators & Grooming Tactics

Online predators **don't always appear dangerous at first**—they often seem kind, understanding, and supportive. They use social media, gaming platforms, and chat apps to **manipulate young girls** into trusting them before taking advantage.

What is Grooming?

Grooming is a slow and calculated process that predators use to **gain trust and control** over their victims. It can happen over days, weeks, or even months.

Stages of Grooming

1 **Building Trust** – They pretend to be a friend, mentor, or someone who understands you.
2 **Gathering Personal Information** – They ask about your family, school, hobbies, and insecurities.

3 **Creating Emotional Dependence** – They shower you with attention, compliments, and gifts.
4 **Isolating You** – They convince you to keep your conversations a secret.
5 **Exploiting & Blackmailing** – They pressure you into sending private photos, meeting in person, or doing something against your will.

Warning Signs of Online Grooming

Someone is **overly interested** in your personal life.
They ask for **private photos** or video calls in secrecy.
They insist on **meeting in person** but want it to be a secret.
They send **gifts or money** for no reason.
They **guilt-trip** you if you refuse to do something.

How to Protect Yourself from Online Predators

Don't Share Personal Details – Never give out your full name, school, or location.
Never Send Private Photos – Anything you send online can be saved or used against you later.
Be Cautious of Overly Friendly Strangers – If someone is too nice too fast, be suspicious.
Tell a Trusted Adult – If something feels wrong, seek help immediately.
Use Strong Privacy Settings – Make sure only trusted people can see your posts and messages.

3. Identity Theft & Impersonation Scams
Ever heard of someone **losing control of their social media account** or finding a fake profile using their name and pictures? **That's identity theft.**

Scammers steal personal information to **impersonate victims, commit fraud, or blackmail them.**

Common Identity Theft Tactics

Fake Profiles – Scammers create social media accounts using your photos and name.
Phishing Attacks – Fake messages or emails trick you into giving away login details.
Hacked Accounts – If someone steals your password, they can use your account to scam others.
Financial Fraud – Scammers can use stolen data to open fake bank accounts or demand money.

Dangers of Identity Theft

Fake profiles can be used to **scam your friends**.
Hackers can post **inappropriate content** from your account.
Stolen personal data can be used for **blackmail or cyberstalking**.
Your **online reputation** could be permanently damaged.

How to Protect Yourself from Identity Theft

Use Strong Passwords & Enable Two-Factor Authentication (2FA).
Don't Click on Suspicious Links or Share OTPs (One-Time Passwords).
Avoid Oversharing Personal Details like your birthday, phone number, or home address.
Regularly Search Your Name Online to check for fake profiles.
If Your Account Gets Hacked, Report It Immediately.

---

4. Privacy Violations & Data Tracking

You might not realize it, but every time you go online, **your data is being tracked.** Social media platforms, advertisers, and even hackers **collect and use** your personal information.

How Your Data Is Collected

20

Social Media Activity – Everything you like, comment on, or search for is recorded.
Location Tracking – Apps track your location unless you disable GPS permissions.
Cookies & Ads – Websites store your data and target you with personalized ads.
Photo Metadata – Your pictures may contain location and device details unless removed.

How Privacy Violations Affect You

Companies **sell your personal data** to advertisers.
Strangers can **track your location** if GPS is enabled.
Hackers can **steal your private information** through weak security settings.
Scammers can use your details for **fraud or blackmail**.

How to Protect Your Privacy

Adjust Your Privacy Settings – Keep profiles private and limit who sees your posts.
Turn Off Location Sharing – Don't post your real-time location online.
Be Careful with Third-Party Apps – Some apps secretly collect your data.
Review Permissions – Disable unnecessary access (e.g., microphone, camera).
Think Before You Post – Once something is online, it's **almost impossible to erase.**

Final Thoughts
Social media is a powerful tool—but it can also be **dangerous if used carelessly**. Cyberbullying, online predators, identity theft, and privacy violations are very real threats, but **they can be avoided** with the right knowledge and precautions.

Stay cautious, think before you click, and always trust your instincts. Your safety and privacy should always come first.

Chapter 3: Securing Your Social Media Accounts

How to Protect Your Accounts from Hackers & Scammers

Social media is a powerful tool, but without the right security measures, it can become a gateway for hackers, scammers, and identity thieves. Just like you wouldn't leave your house unlocked, you shouldn't leave your online accounts vulnerable.

This chapter will walk you through essential steps to **strengthen your passwords, enable two-factor authentication (2FA), adjust privacy settings, and recognize hacking attempts**—so you can stay in control of your digital security.

1. Creating Strong Passwords & Enabling Two-Factor Authentication (2FA)

Why Weak Passwords Are Dangerous

Using a weak password is like giving a hacker an open invitation to your account. Many cybercriminals use stolen or guessed passwords to access social media, emails, and even banking accounts.

A strong password should be:

At least **12-16 characters** long

A mix of **uppercase & lowercase letters, numbers, and symbols**

Not related to personal info (e.g., your name, birthday, pet's name)

Unique for each account (never reuse passwords)

Examples of Weak Passwords:

Emma2005 → Too short and predictable

password123 → One of the most hacked passwords

iloveyou → Very common and easy to guess

Examples of Strong Passwords:

J3$&gY*9x@Pz!4Qw (Random, difficult to guess)

M0on!L1ght#F0x82 (Easy to remember but still complex)

Pro Tip: Use a **password manager** to securely store and generate strong passwords.

How to Enable Two-Factor Authentication (2FA)

Even if someone steals your password, **two-factor authentication (2FA)** ensures they can't log in without a second verification step.

Types of 2FA:

Text Message Codes (SMS) → A temporary code is sent to your phone.

Authentication Apps (More Secure) → Google Authenticator or Authy generate security codes.

Biometric Security → Fingerprint or facial recognition.

How to Turn on 2FA for Popular Platforms:

Instagram: Settings → Security → Two-Factor Authentication

Facebook: Settings → Security & Login → Two-Factor Authentication

TikTok: Settings → Security → 2-Step Verification

Snapchat: Settings → Two-Factor Authentication → Enable

Security Tip: Always choose an authentication app instead of SMS when possible. **Hackers can steal SMS codes through SIM swapping.**

---

2. Adjusting Privacy Settings on Social Media

Your social media accounts store **personal details, photos, locations, and private conversations.** Without the right privacy settings, strangers—or hackers—can access this information.

How to Lock Down Your Privacy on Popular Platforms

Facebook:
Set posts to **Friends Only** (Settings → Privacy)
Turn off **Location Sharing**
Restrict **Friend Requests** to "Friends of Friends"
Disable **Face Recognition**

Instagram:
Set your account to **Private** (Settings → Privacy)
Turn off **Activity Status** (hides when you're online)
Restrict or block unwanted followers

TikTok:
Make your account **Private** (Settings → Privacy)
Disable **Downloads** (prevents people from saving your videos)
Turn off **Location Tracking**

Snapchat:
Enable **Ghost Mode** (hides your location on Snap Map)
Set "Who Can Contact Me?" to **Friends Only**
Disable **Quick Add** to prevent strangers from adding you

WhatsApp:
Set **Last Seen & Profile Photo** to **Contacts Only**
Enable **Disappearing Messages** for extra privacy
Turn on **Fingerprint/Face Unlock** for added security

Bonus Tip: Do a **privacy check every 3 months** to update your settings as social media platforms change their policies.

---

3. How to Spot & Avoid Hacking & Phishing Scams
What Is Phishing?

Phishing is when **scammers pretend to be a trusted company (like Instagram or PayPal) to trick you into revealing your password, personal data, or bank details.**

Red Flags of a Phishing Scam:
A fake email or message claiming to be from Instagram, saying, *"Your account will be deleted unless you verify your login."*
Urgent messages pressuring you to act fast: *"Click this link NOW to recover your account!"*
Suspicious links or attachments.
Emails with **typos, weird formatting, or unusual greetings.**

How to Stay Safe from Phishing & Hacking
Never click on suspicious links—always check the sender before opening emails or DMs.
Verify website URLs—fake sites look real but have slightly different spellings (e.g., *faceb00k.com* instead of *facebook.com*).
Use a password manager—this prevents you from accidentally entering your login info on fake sites.
Enable 2FA—even if someone steals your password, they can't log in without a second verification step.
Keep your apps and software updated—security updates fix weaknesses that hackers exploit.

What to Do If You Get Hacked:
Step 1: Change your password immediately.
Step 2: Enable two-factor authentication (2FA) if you haven't already.
Step 3: Check your account activity (Settings → Security → Login History).
Step 4: Log out from all devices.

Step 5: Report the issue to the platform (Facebook, Instagram, etc.).

Step 6: Warn your friends—hackers often use compromised accounts to scam others.

Final Thoughts: Stay Smart, Stay Safe

The internet is full of risks, but with the right precautions, you can **protect your accounts, personal data, and privacy.**

Your Social Media Security Checklist:

Create **strong, unique passwords** for every account.
Enable **two-factor authentication (2FA)** on all platforms.
Adjust **privacy settings** to limit who can see your content.
Stay alert for **hacking & phishing scams**.
Regularly update your security settings & review account activity.

Remember: Social media should be a fun and safe space. By staying informed and using the right security measures, **you can enjoy the digital world without fear!**

Chapter 4: Safe Communication & Digital Boundaries

Staying Safe Online: Recognizing Red Flags & Protecting Your Privacy

The internet is a powerful tool for communication, but it also comes with risks. While social media helps us stay connected, it exposes us to dangers such as **scams, harassment, blackmail, identity theft, and cyberstalking**.

This chapter will guide you on how to:
Recognize red flags in online conversations
Avoid oversharing personal information
Handle unwanted messages, harassment, and blackmail

By learning how to set digital boundaries and protect your privacy, you can enjoy the online world safely and confidently.

---

1. Recognizing Red Flags in Online Conversations

Not everyone online is who they claim to be. Some people **use fake identities** to manipulate, scam, or exploit others.

Warning Signs of a Suspicious Person

They ask personal questions too soon → Example: *"Where do you live?"* or *"Are you home alone?"*
They refuse video calls or in-person meetings → They might be hiding their true identity.
They seem "too perfect" → Scammers often use fake stories and excessive flattery to gain trust.
They pressure you for photos or personal details → This can be a sign of grooming or blackmail.
They try to isolate you → If someone asks you to *"keep this a secret,"* be cautious.
They send suspicious links → Clicking on unknown links can expose you to scams or hacking.

They talk about money → Romance scammers often invent emotional stories to ask for financial help.

What to Do If You Notice Red Flags:

Stop responding → Don't engage with the person.
Block & report them → Most platforms allow you to report suspicious accounts.
Tell someone you trust → A parent, teacher, or friend can offer advice.
Never send private photos or personal info → Once shared, it can be used against you.

---

2. How to Avoid Oversharing Personal Information
Many people unknowingly share too much online, making it easier for hackers, scammers, and stalkers to take advantage.

Information You Should NEVER Share Online:

Full Name & Address → Avoid posting your home location or school name.
Phone Number & Email → Strangers can use this for scams or hacking attempts.
Passwords & Login Details → Even sharing with close friends can be risky.
Location or Check-Ins → Don't tag your real-time location in posts.
Travel Plans → Posting about vacations makes you a target for burglars.
Private Photos & Videos → Once something is online, you lose control over it.

How to Share Safely:

Use Privacy Settings → Limit who can see your posts and personal details.
Think Before You Post → If you wouldn't tell a stranger, don't

post it online.

Use Fake Birthdates on Public Profiles → Prevents identity theft.
Turn Off Location Services → Apps like Snapchat and Instagram track your location by default.

---

3. Handling Unwanted Messages, Harassment & Blackmail

Online harassment and blackmail are **serious issues** that can cause stress and fear. Here's how to handle them:

A. Dealing with Unwanted Messages & Harassment

Repeated, unwanted messages → Someone keeps messaging you even after you ask them to stop.
Inappropriate comments or threats → Any message that makes you feel uncomfortable.
Spreading false rumors → Cyberbullies may try to damage your reputation.

What to Do:

Ignore & Don't Engage → Responding can escalate the situation.
Block the User → Most platforms let you block unwanted contacts.
Report to the Platform → Facebook, Instagram, TikTok, etc., have reporting options.
Tell Someone You Trust → Parents, teachers, or friends can help.
Keep Evidence → Take screenshots in case you need to report the harassment later.

B. What to Do If Someone Tries to Blackmail You

Online blackmail happens when someone **threatens to release private photos, videos, or information unless you comply with their demands.**

Red Flags of Online Blackmail:

They claim to have private photos of you → Even if you never sent any, scammers may lie.
They demand money or more photos → Never give in to their demands.
They threaten to share things with your family/friends → A common scare tactic.

What to Do:

Do NOT respond to the blackmailer → Any response can make things worse.
Block & report them immediately → Most platforms take action against blackmailers.
Tell someone you trust → A trusted adult or authority can guide you.
Contact the police if necessary → If you feel in danger, report it to law enforcement.
Check your accounts for security breaches → Change your passwords and enable 2FA.

Final Thoughts: Stay Alert & Stay Safe

The best way to **protect yourself online** is to set **clear digital boundaries** and **stay cautious** in online interactions.

Your Online Safety Checklist:

Recognize red flags in conversations.
Be careful about what you share online.
Know how to handle harassment and blackmail.
Use strong passwords & enable two-factor authentication.
Regularly update your privacy settings.

Remember: The internet can be a great place, but only when you stay informed and take the right precautions. **If something feels wrong, trust your instincts and take action!**

Chapter 5: Dealing with Cyberbullying – A Guide to Protecting Yourself

Cyberbullying is one of the most common dangers on social media. Unlike traditional bullying, it happens online and can reach victims **anytime, anywhere**. Learning how to **identify cyberbullying, respond effectively, and seek support** can help you stay strong and safe.

---

1. Identifying Different Types of Cyberbullying

Cyberbullying comes in many forms, some more obvious than others. Here are the most common types:

Harassment & Repeated Messaging

Sending insulting, threatening, or mean messages repeatedly.
Flooding someone's inbox with unwanted messages to intimidate them.
Spamming or trolling in comments or group chats.

Example: Someone keeps sending you hate messages on Instagram, even after you ask them to stop.

Public Humiliation & Shaming

Sharing private or embarrassing photos/videos of someone.
Posting false rumors or insults to damage a person's reputation.
Creating polls, pages, or memes to mock someone.

Example: A fake TikTok account posts edited videos making fun of someone's looks.

Impersonation & Fake Accounts

Pretending to be someone else to trick, humiliate, or harass them.
Creating fake profiles to spread lies or send harmful messages.
Hacking an account to send rude messages under someone's name.

Example: A bully creates a fake Facebook profile with your name and posts false status updates to embarrass you.

Exclusion & Social Manipulation

Deliberately leaving someone out of group chats, online games, or social media groups.
Encouraging others to ignore or block a person.
Secretly talking behind someone's back in private groups.

Example: A group of classmates creates a WhatsApp group but leaves one person out to make them feel isolated.

Doxxing & Threats

Sharing someone's private information (address, phone number, school) online.
Sending violent threats or encouraging self-harm.
Posting personal photos or videos without consent.

Example: Someone posts your address online and encourages others to harass you.

2. How to Respond, Block, and Report Abuse
A. Responding to Cyberbullying

Stay calm & don't react emotionally → Bullies want a reaction.
Avoid arguing with the bully → Engaging can escalate the

situation.

Save evidence → Take screenshots before blocking or deleting messages.

Tell someone you trust → Talk to a parent, teacher, or friend.

Use privacy settings → Make your social media accounts private to limit access.

Example: If someone posts hurtful comments, take screenshots and report them instead of replying.

B. Blocking & Reporting Cyberbullies

Most social media platforms allow you to **block and report bullies**. Here's how:

Instagram → Go to their profile → Tap the three dots → Select *Block & Report.*

Facebook → Tap the three dots on their profile → Click *Block.*

TikTok → Hold down on the comment → Click *Report.*

Snapchat → Tap on their profile → Select *Block & Report.* Use *Ghost Mode* to prevent location tracking.

WhatsApp → Open the chat → Tap their name → Scroll down & select *Block & Report.*

Pro Tip: If cyberbullying includes threats or serious harassment, report it to **law enforcement or your school.**

3. Emotional Coping Strategies & Seeking Support

A. Managing Your Emotions

Cyberbullying can be emotionally draining, but **you have the power to protect your well-being.**

Don't take it personally → Bullies project their own insecurities.

Limit screen time → Taking a break from social media can help.

Write down your feelings → Journaling or talking to someone can relieve stress.

Focus on self-care → Engage in activities you enjoy (music, art, sports, reading).

Example: If a bully keeps sending you messages, log off social media for a while and do something that makes you happy.

B. Seeking Help & Support

You **don't have to go through this alone.** There are people who care about you and want to help.

Talk to someone you trust → A parent, sibling, teacher, or counselor.
Join support groups → Talking to others with similar experiences can be healing.
Seek professional help if needed → If cyberbullying affects your mental health, consider therapy.

Remember: You are NOT alone. Support is always available!

Final Thoughts: You Have the Power to Stay Safe
Your Cyberbullying Protection Plan

Recognize different types of cyberbullying
Respond calmly & save evidence
Block & report the bully immediately
Talk to someone you trust
Take care of your mental health

No one deserves to be bullied. If you or someone you know is being cyberbullied, **take action and seek support.**

Chapter 6: Protecting Your Privacy – What Not to Share & How to Stay Safe

The internet **never forgets**—what you post online can be stored, shared, and misused. Protecting your **personal information, digital footprint, and online reputation** is crucial for staying safe. Here's how to **avoid oversharing, understand digital footprints, and prevent doxxing and hacking.**

---

1. What NOT to Share Online

Some information should **never** be shared online because it can put your **privacy, safety, and security** at risk.

Personal Information to Keep Private

Full Name & Address – Avoid posting your home address or school location.
Phone Number & Email – These can be used for scams or hacking.
Birthdate & Social Security Number – Can be used for identity theft.
Passwords & Security Questions – Even sharing with friends is risky.
Bank Account & Payment Details – Never share financial information online.
Family & Friends' Information – Sharing their details can also put them at risk.

Example: If you post, *"Excited for my trip! Leaving my house empty for a week!"*—this can make you a target for burglary.

Photos & Videos That Can Be Risky

Private or revealing photos – Once shared, you lose control over them.
School uniform or workplace logos – Reveals your location and daily routine.
Party or drinking photos – Can harm your reputation later.
License plates, IDs, or documents – Can be used for fraud.
Screenshots of private conversations – Can be used against you.

Example: Someone might **edit or misuse** your picture to create **fake accounts or blackmail you.**

Location Sharing Dangers

Real-time location (Check-ins, Stories, Live Videos) – Makes it easy for stalkers to track you.
Tagged locations in posts – Shows where you are, making you vulnerable.
Public events or plans – Strangers can find out where to meet you.

What to Do Instead:
✔ Turn off **location tracking** on social media apps.
✔ **Post vacation photos after you return.**
✔ Use **fake or general locations** instead of real ones.

Example: Instead of tagging *"Central Park, NYC,"* use *"Out and about in the city!"*

---

2. Understanding Digital Footprints & Online Reputation
What is a Digital Footprint?

Your **digital footprint** is the **trail of data** you leave behind when using the internet. This includes:
Social media posts, comments, and likes.
Search history and websites visited.

Online purchases and transactions.
Apps and games linked to your accounts.

Example: Employers and colleges check **digital footprints**. A bad post from years ago could hurt your **future opportunities.**

How to Protect Your Online Reputation

Think before you post – Would you be okay if your **family or boss** saw this?
Use privacy settings – Set accounts to **private** and limit who can see your posts.
Delete old, embarrassing posts – Clean up your online presence.
Google yourself – See what **information** is available about you.
Use different usernames – Don't use your **real name** in every account.

Example: A tweet you posted when you were **14 years old** could **come back to haunt you** during a job interview. Be mindful of what you post!

---

3. How to Prevent Doxxing & Hacking

Doxxing is when someone finds and **exposes your personal information** (address, phone number, email, etc.) online to harass or threaten you.

How Hackers & Doxxers Get Your Info

Social media oversharing – Posting too many **personal details.**
Weak passwords – Easy-to-guess passwords like *"123456"* or *"password."*
Public data leaks – Websites you use get **hacked, exposing your details.**
Clicking on phishing links – Fake emails or messages tricking you into **giving passwords.**

Steps to Prevent Doxxing & Hacking

1. Strengthen Your Security

✔ **Use strong passwords** – At least **12 characters** with a mix of **letters, numbers, and symbols.**
✔ **Enable Two-Factor Authentication (2FA)** – Adds extra **security** to logins.
✔ **Avoid using the same password** for multiple accounts.
✔ **Update passwords regularly** – Change them every few months.

Example: Instead of using *"Sarah1234"*, try *"S@r@h!983#_X."*

2. Control Your Privacy Settings

✔ **Set social media accounts to private.**
✔ **Restrict who can tag you** in posts or see your **friends list.**
✔ **Disable location sharing** in apps.

Example: On Instagram, go to **Settings → Privacy → Limit** who can see your content.

3. Avoid Clicking on Phishing Links

✔ **Never open random links** in emails or DMs – Always **verify first.**
✔ **Be cautious of "urgent" messages** – Scammers try to create **panic.**
✔ **Check for spelling errors** in website links – Fake sites **look real** but have slight **spelling mistakes.**

Example: A scam email may say *"Your account is at risk! Click here to reset your password!"*—but it's a **fake link.**

4. Remove Personal Information from Public Sites

✔ **Google yourself** and **request removal** of sensitive data.
✔ **Use a fake name or nickname** for **non-essential accounts.**
✔ **Avoid filling out unnecessary online forms** that ask for personal info.

Example: If a website asks for your **real phone number,** use a **secondary or fake number** instead.

Final Thoughts: Be Smart & Stay Safe!
Your Online Privacy Checklist

Never share personal details online.
Think before posting – Your **digital footprint** lasts forever.
Use strong passwords & enable 2FA.
Be cautious of phishing scams & suspicious links.
Adjust privacy settings on social media.

Online safety is in YOUR hands! If you're unsure about something, **pause, think, and protect yourself.**

Chapter 7: Smart Social Media Habits for Girls
Managing Screen Time, Avoiding Misinformation & Protecting Mental Health

Social media can be a great tool for connection, learning, and entertainment—but if not used wisely, it can lead to addiction, misinformation, and mental health struggles. Understanding how to balance screen time, recognize fake news, and maintain a healthy mindset is key to using social media safely and positively.

---

1. Managing Screen Time & Social Media Addiction

Social media apps are designed to keep us scrolling for hours, making it easy to lose track of time. But excessive screen time can negatively impact sleep, focus, productivity, and mental well-being.

Signs of Social Media Addiction

- Feeling anxious or restless when not using social media.
- Constantly checking notifications, even during important tasks.
- Spending hours scrolling without realizing it.
- Using social media to escape real-life problems.
- Losing interest in hobbies or real-life interactions.

Example: If you reach for your phone the moment you wake up and feel uneasy without it, you might be too dependent on social media.

Tips to Reduce Screen Time & Take Control

✔ **Set Time Limits** – Use app timers (on iPhone or Android) to limit daily usage.
✔ **Create Social Media-Free Zones** – No phones during meals, study/work hours, or bedtime.

✔ **Turn Off Unnecessary Notifications** – Fewer alerts = Less temptation to check.

✔ **Replace Scrolling with Other Activities** – Read a book, exercise, or spend time with friends.

✔ **Take Digital Detox Days** – Try going offline for a day each week.

Example: Set a rule like *"No social media after 9 PM"* to improve sleep and mental clarity.

Self-Reflection Questions:

- How much time do I spend on social media daily?

- Does social media interfere with my sleep or responsibilities?

- How do I feel after spending a lot of time online?

2. Recognizing Fake News, Misinformation & Deepfakes

The internet is full of misleading information, from fake news articles to altered images and deepfake videos. Learning to fact-check can protect you from being misled.

How to Spot Fake News & Misinformation

Clickbait Headlines – Sensational or exaggerated titles that aim to shock you.

Unverified Sources – No official websites or credible sources linked.

Emotional Manipulation – Tries to make you angry, scared, or excited to share quickly.

Photoshopped Images & Misused Videos – Out-of-context or edited media.

No Author or Date – Reliable news sources always mention who wrote the article and when it was published.

Example: A viral post claims *"Instagram will delete your account if you don't share this!"* – but no official Instagram page confirms this.

How to Detect Deepfakes (Fake Videos & AI-Generated Content)

Look for Unnatural Eye Movements – Deepfakes struggle to make blinking look natural.
Check the Lips & Voice Sync – If lips don't match the words, it might be fake.
Reverse Image Search – Upload a screenshot to Google Images to check if it's been altered.
Fact-Check with Trusted News Outlets – CNN, BBC, Reuters, and sites like Snopes can verify information.

Example: A deepfake video of a celebrity endorsing a scam investment scheme—always verify from official sources before believing or sharing.

Self-Reflection Questions:

- Have I ever believed and shared misinformation?
- How do I verify if something is real before sharing it?
- What sources do I trust for news, and are they credible?

---

3. The Impact of Social Media on Self-Esteem & Mental Health

Social media can boost confidence when used positively, but it can also lead to comparison, low self-esteem, and anxiety.

Negative Effects of Social Media on Mental Health

Comparison Trap – Seeing others' "perfect" lives makes people feel inadequate.
Fear of Missing Out (FOMO) – Feeling left out when you see

friends having fun without you.

Cyberbullying & Hate Comments – Hurtful messages can impact self-esteem.

Unrealistic Beauty Standards – Edited images create false ideas about beauty.

Social Validation Addiction – Feeling self-worth depends on likes, comments, and followers.

Example: A girl sees influencers with perfect bodies on Instagram and starts feeling insecure, not realizing those images are edited and filtered.

How to Maintain a Healthy Relationship with Social Media

✔ **Follow Positive & Uplifting Accounts** – Unfollow pages that make you feel bad.

✔ **Remember: Social Media is Not Reality** – Most people only post the best parts of their lives.

✔ **Limit Comparing Yourself to Others** – Focus on your own progress and achievements.

✔ **Take Breaks When Feeling Overwhelmed** – Step away from social media when it affects your mood.

✔ **Surround Yourself with Real-Life Support** – Spend more time with family, friends, and hobbies that bring real joy.

Example: Instead of stressing over not having as many followers as someone else, focus on what makes you happy offline.

Self-Reflection Questions:

- How does social media affect my self-esteem?

- Do I compare myself to others online? How can I stop?

- What are three things I love about myself that social media doesn't define?

Your Social Media Wellness Plan:

Set time limits & avoid overuse.
Think critically before believing or sharing news.
Watch out for deepfakes & scams.
Protect your mental health & avoid negative comparisons.
Take breaks & focus on real-life happiness.

Social media is a powerful tool—use it wisely to uplift yourself, not bring yourself down! ✦

Bonus: Step-by-Step Guide to Managing Screen Time, Fact-Checking News & Detecting Deepfakes

How to Set Screen Time Limits on Your Phone & Apps
iPhone Users:
1 Go to **Settings** → Tap **Screen Time**.
2 Turn on **Screen Time** if it's not enabled.
3 Tap **App Limits** → Choose social media apps → Set daily time limits.

Android Users:
1 Go to **Settings** → Tap **Digital Wellbeing & Parental Controls**.
2 Tap **Dashboard** → Select the app you want to limit.

How to Fact-Check News & Avoid Misinformation
1 **Verify the Source** – Is it from a reliable news outlet?
2 **Cross-Check with Fact-Checking Websites** like Snopes & PolitiFact.
3 **Check the Date & Context** – Is it old news being reshared?

How to Detect Deepfakes
Look for unnatural blinking & facial movements.
Use **Deepware Scanner** or **Reality Defender** to analyze videos.

Your Social Media Safety Checklist:
Set screen time limits – Don't let social media control your time.
Verify news before sharing – Use fact-checking sites & reverse image search.
Be skeptical of deepfakes – Use detection tools & analyze videos carefully.
Use privacy & security tools – Protect your personal data.
Take regular digital detoxes – Balance online & offline life.

By following these steps, you can **stay informed, protect your mental well-being, and avoid online scams.** 💡

Recognizing Phishing Attempts & Financial Scams: How to Stay Safe Online

The internet is full of scams, fake giveaways, and phishing attacks designed to steal your money, personal details, or financial information. Learning how to recognize red flags and protect yourself is essential for safe online transactions.

---

1. Recognizing Phishing Attempts & Financial Scams

Phishing is when scammers pretend to be a trusted company or person to trick you into giving up sensitive information (passwords, credit card details, etc.).

Common Phishing Scams

Fake Emails from Banks/Companies – Scammers send emails pretending to be from PayPal, Amazon, or banks, asking you to "verify your account."

Fraudulent Job Offers – Scammers offer fake jobs that require you to pay upfront for training or work materials.

Government or Tax Scams – Fake messages pretending to be from the IRS, Social Security, or local tax authorities demanding money.

Tech Support Scams – Fake pop-ups saying "Your computer has a virus," urging you to call a number for "support."

Romance & Investment Scams – Online scammers pretend to be in love or offer fake investment opportunities to steal money.

Example: You receive an email saying *"Your PayPal account has been suspended! Click here to restore access."* But the link goes to a fake PayPal website designed to steal your login details.

How to Spot a Phishing Scam

Suspicious Email Address – Fake emails come from addresses like "support@paypal-security.com" instead of **support@paypal.com**.
Urgency & Fear Tactics – Scammers pressure you with messages like *"Your account will be deleted in 24 hours!"*
Suspicious Links – Hover over links (without clicking) to check the actual URL.
Grammar & Spelling Mistakes – Official companies use professional communication.
Unexpected Attachments – Legitimate companies never send attachments in emails.

Example: A text message says *"Your bank account has been locked! Click here to unlock."* But your bank never sends messages with clickable links!

Self-Reflection Questions:

- Have I ever received an email that seemed suspicious? What did I do?

- How can I verify if an email is really from my bank or a company?

- What steps do I take to protect my passwords and financial accounts?

2. How to Avoid Fake Giveaways & Suspicious Links
Spotting Fake Giveaways on Social Media

Many scammers pretend to give away free iPhones, luxury bags, or cash to steal personal information.

Red Flags of Fake Giveaways:
"Like, Share & Comment to Win" Giveaways – Many fake giveaways ask you to engage with their post to spread the scam.
Fake Celebrity or Brand Accounts – Scammers impersonate real influencers and brands (check for verified blue ticks).
Asking for Payment – Legitimate giveaways NEVER ask for shipping fees or entry payments.

Links to Unknown Websites – If a giveaway doesn't come from the brand's official website, it's a scam.

Example: A page claims *"Amazon is giving away 100 iPhones for free! Click the link to enter."* But the link leads to a scam website that steals your personal data.

How to Identify Suspicious Links

Check the URL Carefully – Fake websites often have slight spelling errors (e.g., "amaz0n.com" instead of "amazon.com").
Use Link Checkers – Tools like <u>VirusTotal</u> or Google Safe Browsing can scan URLs for scams.
Look for HTTPS – Secure websites start with "https://", but even fake sites can have HTTPS, so always double-check!
Don't Click on Shortened Links – Scammers use services like bit.ly to hide real URLs.

Example: A Twitter giveaway says *"Win $1000! Click bit.ly/FreeCash to claim."* But the shortened link leads to a fake survey scam.

Self-Reflection Questions:

- Have I ever entered a giveaway without checking if it was real?
- How can I verify if a giveaway or contest is legitimate?
- What are three steps I can take to avoid clicking on scam links?

---

3. Protecting Your Online Shopping & Payment Information

Safe Online Shopping Practices

Shop Only on Trusted Websites – Stick to official brand websites or reputable online marketplaces.
Check Reviews & Seller Ratings – If a product has zero reviews or looks too good to be true, it's likely a scam.

Avoid Deals That Seem Unrealistic – If a $2000 laptop is selling for $100, it's probably fake.

Never Enter Your Credit Card Details on Pop-Ups – Secure websites never ask for payments outside the checkout page.

Example: You see an ad for Nike shoes at 90% off, but the website is **"NikeStoreDiscount.com"** instead of the real **Nike.com**—this is a scam.

How to Secure Your Payment Information Online

✔ **Use Virtual Cards or PayPal** – Many banks offer temporary virtual cards for online purchases.

✔ **Enable Two-Factor Authentication (2FA)** – Add extra security to your banking and shopping accounts.

✔ **Monitor Your Bank Statements Regularly** – Watch out for unauthorized transactions.

✔ **Don't Save Your Card Details on Websites** – If the site gets hacked, your info is at risk.

Example: You buy a phone case online and save your card details, but later, hackers steal the website's data and access your card.

Self-Reflection Questions:

- How do I ensure a website is safe before making a purchase?

- Have I ever fallen for a fake online deal? What did I learn?

- How can I better protect my financial information online?

Final Checklist: Stay Safe from Online Scams & Phishing Attacks

Before Clicking a Link or Entering Personal Info, Ask Yourself:

Is the email or message from a verified sender?
Does the website URL look suspicious or have spelling mistakes?

Is the offer "too good to be true"?
Did I receive this message unexpectedly?
Is someone asking me to pay fees for a giveaway?
Does the site have reviews or trust signals?

By following these precautionary steps, you can avoid falling victim to online scams and phishing attacks. Stay cautious, think critically, and protect yourself in the digital world! 🛡💡

Chapter 9: Romance Scams – The Dangers of Online Love

How Scammers Manipulate Emotions & Gain Trust

Scammers are experts at playing with emotions to make their victims trust them. They use psychological tricks to make you feel loved, safe, or pressured, leading you to send them money or personal information.

---

1. How Scammers Manipulate Emotions & Gain Trust

Love Bombing

Scammers shower their victims with compliments, attention, and promises of love.
They say things like *"I've never met anyone like you"* or *"We're soulmates,"* often too soon in the relationship.
This makes victims emotionally attached and less likely to question things.

Example: A scammer you met online tells you *"I love you"* after just a few days and starts calling you *"my soulmate."*

Fake Urgency & Emotional Pressure

Scammers create emergencies to make victims feel guilty or scared into sending money quickly.
Common excuses:

- *"My mother is sick, and I need money for her surgery."*

- *"I got arrested in a foreign country, and I need bail money."*

- *"My bank account is frozen, and I can't access my salary!"*

Example: After chatting for weeks, your online "boyfriend" suddenly says he needs $500 for a visa to visit you.

Pretending to be in the Military or a Businessperson

Many scammers pretend to be soldiers, doctors, or engineers working overseas.
They claim to be in dangerous war zones or on secret missions so they can't meet in person.
This makes victims feel sympathy and obligated to help.

Example: A scammer says he's a U.S. soldier stationed in Syria and needs money to leave the war zone.

Building Fake Long-Term Trust

Some scammers talk for months before asking for money.
They pretend to be in love, share fake family photos, and even send gifts.
This tricks victims into believing they're in a real relationship.

Example: A woman talks to a scammer online for six months, thinking he's her future husband—until he asks for money for a business investment.

Self-Reflection Questions:

- Have I ever received overly affectionate messages from someone I barely know?

- How can I spot red flags in an online relationship?

- What are three steps I can take to verify if someone online is real?

2. Signs of a Romance Scam & Fake Relationships
Too Much Too Soon – They express deep love immediately, even before meeting in person.

They Avoid Video Calls – They always make excuses when you ask for a video chat.

They Ask for Money – They claim to have a medical emergency, visa issue, or business problem.

They Have a "Perfect" Life – Their stories sound too good to be true (rich, kind, and always "single").

They Live Far Away – They claim to work overseas, in the military, or on a special mission.

They Ask for Personal Information – They want details like your bank account, address, or ID number.

Their Social Media Looks Fake – Their profile has few photos, few friends, and was recently created.

Example: You meet a *"wealthy businessman"* online, but when you reverse-search his profile picture, it appears on many scam reports.

Self-Reflection Questions:

- Have I ever ignored warning signs because I wanted to believe in love?

- How can I verify if someone's identity is real?

- What would I do if an online friend suddenly asked for money?

---

3. True Stories of Victims & How to Escape Such Traps

Case 1: The Fake Military Boyfriend Scam

What Happened?
Sarah, 35, met *"John,"* a U.S. soldier stationed overseas.
He sent romantic messages every day for three months.
One day, he said he needed $2,000 to fly home.
She sent the money—but he disappeared after that.

How to Avoid This Scam:
Search his name + *"scam"* on Google.

Reverse-image search his photos to see if they belong to someone else.

Never send money to someone you haven't met in real life.

Case 2: The Wealthy Businessman Scam

What Happened?
Emma, 28, met *"David"* on Instagram—a rich-looking investor from Dubai.

He told her she was beautiful and special.

He promised to visit her soon but needed money to unlock his *"frozen account."*

She sent $5,000—but he was a scammer using stolen pictures.

How to Avoid This Scam:
Check if their social media has very few friends or posts.

Refuse to send money, no matter what excuse they give.

If they pressure you for money, block and report them.

Case 3: The Fake Modeling Offer Scam

What Happened?
Mia, 22, got a message from a *"fashion agency"* offering her a modeling job.

They asked for personal details, photos, and a $500 registration fee.

She sent the money—only to realize the agency didn't exist.

How to Avoid This Scam:
Research any company before accepting offers.

Legitimate jobs NEVER ask for money upfront.

Check if the company has an official website and verified contacts.

Self-Reflection Questions:

- Have I ever believed in an online story without verifying it?

- How can I protect myself from being emotionally manipulated?

- If a friend told me they were in an online relationship, what advice would I give them?

4. How to Escape & Report Romance Scams
What to Do If You Suspect a Scammer

Stop Contact Immediately – Block & delete them.
Never Send More Money – If they already scammed you, don't fall for another excuse.
Save the Evidence – Keep screenshots of messages, emails, and receipts.
Warn Others – Report the scammer to:

- **FBI Internet Crime Complaint Center (IC3)** (USA)

- **Scamwatch** (Australia)

- **Action Fraud** (UK)

- **Local Police or Cybercrime Units**

Example: If someone claims to be a rich investor but asks for money, report their Instagram/Facebook profile as a scam.

Final Checklist: Stay Safe from Romance Scams
Before Trusting Someone Online, Ask Yourself:

Have I ever seen them on video chat?
Do they ask for money, gifts, or favors?
Do their social media accounts seem fake?
Are they in a *"distant"* job (military, oil rig, international

business)?
Did I verify their identity with a reverse image search?

By staying alert and following these steps, you can avoid falling victim to romance scams and emotional manipulation. Protect your heart—and your wallet!

Chapter 10: Girls Lured into Prostitution

The Dark Side – How Girls Are Lured into Prostitution & Human Trafficking

Introduction

Social media, while offering endless opportunities to connect and express oneself, has also become a **hunting ground for human traffickers**. These criminals exploit vulnerable girls through **fake job offers, online friendships, romantic relationships, and deceptive promises**. Many victims are manipulated without realizing the danger until it's too late.

This chapter will help **young girls, parents, and educators** understand:
✔ **How traffickers operate on social media**
✔ **Warning signs & recruitment tactics to watch for**
✔ **Real-life stories of victims**
✔ **How to protect yourself and seek help**

1 How Traffickers Use Social Media to Target Girls

Common Tactics Used by Human Traffickers

1 Fake Job Opportunities
"High-paying modeling, acting, or hostess jobs" posted on Instagram or TikTok.
Fake recruiters DM girls with **offers to work abroad** or at luxury events.
Once the girl **accepts, she is asked for personal details** like a passport or address.
Upon arrival, the victim's **documents are confiscated**, and she is **forced into prostitution**.

Example:
A girl receives a message on Instagram:
"Hey gorgeous! We are looking for new models for a fashion shoot in America. Free travel & stay! DM if interested!"
Reality: This is often a **trap** leading to **human trafficking rings**.

2 The "Lover Boy" Scam (Fake Romantic Relationships)

A trafficker **pretends to be a caring boyfriend**.

He **gains the girl's trust** through sweet words, gifts, and promises.

Once emotionally dependent, he **pressures her into prostitution**, claiming it's "just once" or that they need money.

Some victims are **sold to sex traffickers and lose all freedom**.

Example:

A 16-year-old girl meets a guy online. He tells her, *"You're special. I'll take you away from your problems."*

Reality: He isolates her from her family and later forces her into sex work.

3 Fake Friendships & Influencer Traps

Girls are lured with **free trips, VIP parties, or brand promotions**.

Once they arrive at a location, they **lose their freedom**.

Some are **drugged and abducted**, while others are blackmailed.

Example:

A trafficker DMs:

"Hey girl! We're throwing a private influencer party this weekend. Only VIPs! Wanna come?"

Reality: Once there, **the girls are trapped** and **their phones are confiscated**.

4 Sextortion & Blackmail

Traffickers convince girls to **send private photos**.

They later **threaten to expose the pictures** unless the girl obeys them.

Many victims are **forced into prostitution out of fear**.

Example:

A girl shares a private photo with someone she trusts online. The next day, he messages:

"If you don't send more, I'll leak this photo to everyone you

know."
Reality: This is a trap that can lead to trafficking.

---

2 Warning Signs & How to Identify Recruitment Tactics

Red Flags of Traffickers on Social Media

They promise high-paying jobs with no experience required.
They ask for personal details like your ID or passport too soon.
They avoid video calls or meeting in public places.
They push you to travel alone for a "great opportunity."
They send expensive gifts and try to isolate you from friends & family.
They claim to be "in love" too soon and ask for total trust.
They pressure you to keep things a secret.
They ask for inappropriate photos or try to manipulate you emotionally.

---

3 Real-Life Stories & How to Seek Help

Case 1: The Fake Modeling Job

What Happened?

- Lisa, 19, was messaged on Instagram by a **fake modeling agent**.

- He promised a **trip to Paris with a fashion brand**.

- When she arrived, her **passport was taken**, and she was **trapped**.

How Lisa Escaped:
She secretly messaged her family with **her location**.

Her family contacted **the embassy and local police**.
She was **rescued and returned home safely**.

Case 2: The "Loving" Boyfriend Scam

What Happened?

- 16-year-old Sophie met a man online who **showered her with love & gifts**.

- After a few months, he **convinced her to run away** to live with him.

- Once she arrived, he **forced her into prostitution**.

How Sophie Escaped:
A **client noticed she was in distress** and called a **human trafficking hotline**.
Authorities **raided the location** and saved her.

Case 3: The Kidnapping Setup

What Happened?

- 17-year-old Maria was **invited to a "private party"** by an influencer she followed.

- She and her friend **went to the location**—but it was a **trap**.

- The traffickers **locked them in a house & planned to sell them**.

How Maria Escaped:
She **pretended to be sick** and convinced them to let her call a family member.
Her **friend shared their last location on Snapchat before they got**

trapped.
Police rescued them just in time.

---

4 How to Stay Safe & Seek Help

How to Protect Yourself from Human Traffickers

Never accept job offers from strangers online.
Always verify any company before traveling for work.
Never share personal details like address, passport, or ID.
Tell someone you trust where you're going & share your location.
Never meet online "friends" in private places.
If you feel uncomfortable, trust your instincts & leave immediately.
Avoid traveling alone, especially to unknown places.

Example: A girl gets an invite to an influencer's house party. She brings a trusted friend, shares her live location, and keeps emergency contacts ready—just in case.

Where to Seek Help If You or Someone You Know Is at Risk

Emergency Hotlines & Resources:

U.S. National Human Trafficking Hotline: **1-888-373-7888** (Text: HELP to 233733)
UK Modern Slavery Helpline: **08000 121 700**
Canada Human Trafficking Hotline: **1-833-900-1010**
India National Helpline for Women: **1091 / 181**
International NGO Polaris: **www.polarisproject.org**

Example: If a friend is acting strangely and withdrawing from family after meeting someone

Chapter 11: Mental & Emotional Well-Being in the Digital Age

The Social Media Trap – Overcoming FOMO, Anxiety & Digital Detox

Introduction

Social media is designed to keep us scrolling, engaging, and comparing. The fear of missing out (FOMO), social media anxiety, and the pressure to keep up with the perfect-looking lives online can take a toll on mental health.

This chapter will cover:
✔ **How FOMO affects our mental well-being**
✔ **The dangers of social media comparison culture**
✔ **The psychological effects of excessive screen time**
✔ **How to take breaks and regain control with a digital detox**

---

1. Understanding FOMO: The Fear of Missing Out

What is FOMO?

FOMO is the constant fear that others are having more fun, achieving more, or living better lives than you. It's fueled by:
Seeing friends at a party you weren't invited to
Watching influencers travel the world while you're at home
Feeling pressure to stay updated on trends & new experiences

Example: You scroll through Instagram and see your friends at an event. Suddenly, you feel left out and upset—even though you were content before seeing the post.

The Reality?

✔ Most people only post the **best parts** of their lives—not their struggles.
✔ Social media creates an **illusion of perfection**, but it's not real.

✔ Everyone experiences **self-doubt and bad days**, even if they don't post about it.

The Science Behind FOMO
FOMO activates the brain's **dopamine system**, the same mechanism linked to addiction. This makes social media addictive, as every notification, like, or update **triggers a reward response**, keeping users hooked.

How to Overcome FOMO

Practice Gratitude – Focus on what you have instead of what you lack.
Limit Exposure – Take breaks from accounts that trigger FOMO.
Live in the Moment – Engage in real-life experiences instead of obsessing over online ones.

Self-Reflection Exercise:
Write down three moments you felt FOMO. Was the feeling exaggerated by social media? How did you feel after taking a break?

---

2. Dealing with Social Media Anxiety & Comparison Culture
The Dark Side of Social Media

Feeling pressured to look perfect online
Comparing your body, achievements, and lifestyle to influencers
Seeking validation through likes and comments
Feeling unworthy if your post doesn't get enough engagement

Example: A girl sees a fitness influencer with a "perfect body" and feels insecure—without realizing the image is heavily edited and posed.

The Reality?

✔ Many influencers use **filters, Photoshop, and staged photos.**
✔ People post their **best angles, outfits, and moments**—not their daily struggles.
✔ **Social media doesn't define your worth.**

How to Stop Comparing Yourself

Unfollow toxic accounts – If an account makes you feel bad, unfollow or mute it.
Follow real, positive content creators – Engage with uplifting, body-positive, and educational content.
Remind yourself: Social media is NOT real life – A perfect Instagram post doesn't mean a perfect life.

Self-Reflection Exercise:

- List 5 things you love about yourself **that aren't related to social media.**

- How do you feel after reducing time on social platforms?

---

3. The Hidden Dangers of Excessive Screen Time
Social media overuse doesn't just impact self-esteem—it affects overall well-being.

Negative Effects of Too Much Social Media:

- **Anxiety & depression** – Constant comparison lowers self-worth.

- **Sleep problems** – Blue light & late-night scrolling disrupts sleep patterns.

- **Reduced focus & productivity** – Social media shortens attention span.

- **Lower real-life social skills** – Digital addiction makes face-to-face communication harder.

Scientific Insight:
A **University of Pennsylvania study (2018)** found that **reducing social media use to 30 minutes per day** significantly decreased feelings of **loneliness and depression** in just three weeks.

---

4. Digital Detox: How to Take Breaks from Social Media
Too much screen time can leave you feeling:
Drained and unfocused
Disconnected from real life
More anxious and insecure

Signs You Need a Digital Detox

You check your phone **first thing in the morning** & **last thing at night**
You feel **anxious when away from your phone**
You **mindlessly scroll for hours** & feel worse afterward
You **compare yourself** to others constantly

How to Take a Digital Detox

Step 1: Set Screen Time Limits
Use apps like **Digital Wellbeing (Android) or Screen Time (iPhone)** to track and reduce daily usage.

Step 2: Take "No-Social-Media" Days
Try a **social media-free Sunday** or avoid using your phone 1 hour before bed.

Step 3: Turn Off Notifications
Reduce distractions by disabling unnecessary alerts.

Step 4: Replace Scrolling with Real-Life Activities
Instead of spending **3 hours on Instagram**, try:
Reading a book
Exercising

Journaling
Calling a friend

Example: Instead of checking your phone immediately in the morning, stretch, pray, or read a chapter of a book—it will set a positive tone for the day.

---

5. The 7-Day Digital Detox Challenge
Day 1: **Track your screen time** & set reduction goals
Day 2: **No phone for the first & last hour of the day**
Day 3: **Unfollow/mute toxic accounts**
Day 4: **Replace scrolling with a new hobby**
Day 5: **Turn off unnecessary notifications**
Day 6: **Have a social media-free evening**
Day 7: **Reflect: How do you feel? What changed?**

Conclusion: Take Back Control
Social media should be a **tool for connection and inspiration—** not a source of stress and self-doubt.

Key Takeaways:

✔ **Social media is NOT real life**—don't compare yourself to edited highlights.
✔ **You are MORE than your likes, followers, or online presence.**
✔ **Taking breaks from social media improves mental health & happiness.**

Reflection Questions:

- How has social media affected my self-esteem?

- What changes can I make to have a **healthier relationship with social media?**

Chapter 12: Digital Self-Defense Against Online Harassment

Protecting Yourself – Reporting Harassment, Recognizing Manipulation & Digital SOS

Introduction

Online harassment, cyberstalking, and digital abuse are growing threats in the digital age. Many victims feel powerless, but **knowledge is your best defense.** Understanding your rights, gathering evidence, and using digital safety strategies can empower you to **fight back against online abuse.**

This chapter will cover:
✔ **How to document and report online harassment for legal action**
✔ **Recognizing gaslighting, manipulation, and emotional blackmail**
✔ **Setting up emergency contacts and digital SOS strategies**

---

1. Documenting & Reporting Online Harassment for Legal Action

Recognizing Online Harassment

Cyberbullying – Repeated harmful messages, public shaming, or hate speech
Cyberstalking – Unwanted surveillance, tracking, or excessive messaging
Threats & Blackmail – Threatening harm, financial extortion, or revenge porn
Doxxing – Leaking private information (address, phone number) without consent
Impersonation – Fake accounts pretending to be you to spread false info

Ignoring harassment won't stop it. Taking action is key!

Step 1: Gather & Save Evidence

Before confronting or reporting the harasser, **document everything.**
Never delete threatening messages – Take screenshots & record chat logs.
Save profile links – Capture usernames & URLs before the harasser deletes them.
Keep timestamps – Record the date & time of every abusive incident.
Download your social media data – Platforms like Instagram & Facebook allow you to download your activity logs.
Secure sensitive evidence – Store files in a **password-protected folder or cloud storage.**

Example: A girl receives threatening DMs from an anonymous account. Instead of replying, she screenshots the messages, saves the profile link, and reports it to both **social media platforms and authorities.**

Step 2: Report Harassment to Platforms & Authorities

Social Media Platforms
Instagram, Facebook, Twitter, TikTok, and YouTube allow users to **report abusive accounts, messages, and comments.**
Use "Block & Report" instead of just deleting messages.

Legal Authorities & Cybercrime Units
If threats involve stalking, death threats, or revenge porn, report them to local police or cybercrime units.
In many countries, **sharing private photos without consent is illegal.**
Some nations have dedicated **cybercrime hotlines and women's helplines**—use them if you feel unsafe.

Example: A woman receives blackmail threats from an ex. She gathers **evidence, reports the threats to the police, and reaches out to a women's protection service.**

Tip: If law enforcement is unresponsive, seek **legal aid groups** or **digital rights organizations** in your country.

---

2. Understanding Gaslighting, Manipulation & Emotional Blackmail

What is Gaslighting?

Gaslighting is a psychological manipulation tactic where the abuser makes the victim **doubt their own memory, feelings, or reality.**

Common Gaslighting Phrases:
"You're just being dramatic."
"That never happened—you're making things up."
"Nobody will believe you anyway."

How to Fight Gaslighting

Trust your instincts – If something feels wrong, it probably is.
Keep records of conversations – Save messages to validate your experience.
Seek support – Talk to a trusted friend, therapist, or support group.

Example: A girl confronts an online harasser, who responds, *"You're too sensitive. I was just joking."* Instead of doubting herself, she **trusts her feelings, blocks the person, and reports them.**

Emotional Blackmail & Online Manipulation

Some abusers **use threats, guilt, or fear to control their victims.**

Examples of Digital Emotional Blackmail:
Threats – *"If you leave me, I'll ruin your life."*
Guilt-tripping – *"After everything I've done for you, you owe me."*
Financial control – *"You won't survive without my support."*

How to Protect Yourself

Recognize **manipulation tactics** and **refuse to engage.**
Block & remove toxic people from your digital life.
Seek professional support if someone is emotionally controlling you.

Example: A girl breaks up with her boyfriend, but he says, *"If you leave me, I'll hurt myself."* Instead of giving in, she blocks him and **alerts a trusted friend** for support.

Tip: If someone threatens self-harm, **inform their family or a mental health hotline**—but don't feel pressured to stay in a toxic situation.

---

3. Setting Up Emergency Contacts & Digital SOS Strategies
Emergency Contact List

Save trusted **family, friends & helplines** under recognizable names (e.g., **"Emergency Help" instead of just "Mom"**).
Set up ICE (In Case of Emergency) contacts in your phone settings.
Enable location sharing with a trusted contact when traveling alone.

Example: A girl traveling alone shares her live location with a friend for safety.

Digital SOS Strategies for Quick Help

Enable SOS Mode on Your Phone
iPhone: Press the power button **5 times quickly** to send an SOS.
Android: Use Google Personal Safety App or press the **power button 3 times** for emergency alerts.

Set Up a Secret Code with a Friend
A **pre-decided text** like *"Where's my red jacket?"* can signal distress without raising suspicion.

Use Emergency Safety Apps
✔ **bSafe** – Sends emergency alerts & records video/audio.
✔ **Noonlight** – Activates emergency help with a silent alert.
✔ **Life360** – Allows family members to track each other's locations in real-time.

Example: A girl in danger discreetly **presses her phone's SOS button**, which sends her location and an alert to her emergency contacts.

Tip: **Test your emergency apps & settings regularly** to ensure they work when needed.

Conclusion: Stay Informed, Stay Safe
Online harassment can escalate—document and report it.
Gaslighting and manipulation are real—trust your instincts.
Emergency plans save lives—set up digital safety tools.

Key Takeaways:

✔ **Always save evidence of harassment before reporting.**
✔ **If someone manipulates you, seek support and cut off toxic people.**

✔ Set up emergency contacts & learn digital SOS tools for quick help.

Reflection Questions:

- Have I ever ignored online harassment instead of reporting it?

- Do I have emergency contacts & safety measures set up?

- What steps can I take today to improve my digital security?

Bonus: Digital Safety Checklist

Save emergency contacts in your phone
Enable SOS alerts on your phone
Install a personal safety app (bSafe, Life360)
Set up a secret distress signal with a trusted friend
Regularly review social media privacy settings

Chapter 13: The Psychology of Online Predators & Grooming

How They Gain Trust & Manipulate Victims

Introduction

Online predators are **master manipulators** who use deception and psychological tactics to groom their victims—especially **young girls and vulnerable individuals**. Grooming is a **gradual and calculated process** where predators build trust before exploiting their targets.

This chapter will cover:
✔ **How predators gain trust and manipulate victims**
✔ **Warning signs of dangerous online relationships**
✔ **What to do if you or someone you know is being groomed**

1. How Predators Gain Trust & Manipulate Victims
The Grooming Process: Step by Step

Predators **don't immediately reveal their true intentions**. Instead, they take a **step-by-step approach** to gain control.

1. Targeting the Victim

They look for **vulnerable individuals**, such as those who post about feeling lonely, insecure, or misunderstood.
They engage with the victim's posts—**liking, commenting, and messaging** to establish familiarity.

2. Building Friendship & Gaining Trust

They **pretend to be kind, caring, and understanding**, often acting as a supportive friend.
They **compliment**, listen, and provide emotional support to **make**

the victim feel special.
They may **pretend to be the same age** by using **fake profiles.**

3. Isolating the Victim

They **discourage victims from talking** to family & friends.
They **create emotional dependence**, making the victim feel like
they are the only one who "understands" them.
They use **manipulative phrases** like:

- *"No one loves you like I do."*

- *"Your parents wouldn't understand us."*

- *"We have something special—don't let others ruin it."*

4. Testing Boundaries & Normalizing Harmful Behavior

They **gradually** introduce inappropriate topics, personal
questions, or **sexual discussions.**
They **desensitize the victim** by making inappropriate jokes or
sending explicit content.
They **encourage secrecy**:

- *"This is just between us."*

- *"It's normal, everyone does this."*

5. Exploiting & Controlling

They **demand inappropriate pictures/videos** or **pressure victims**
into real-life meetings.
They **use blackmail**:

- *"If you don't send more, I'll leak your photos."*
  They **threaten, guilt-trip, or manipulate** the victim into compliance.

Example: A 15-year-old girl meets a guy online who seems sweet
and understanding. Over time, he asks for personal photos, then
starts demanding explicit content while **threatening to expose**
their conversations if she refuses.

The Reality?

Predators don't always look scary—they can **seem charming, supportive, and fun.**
Many predators pretend to be teenagers using **fake profiles.**
Most victims don't realize they are being groomed until it's too late.

---

2. Warning Signs of Dangerous Online Relationships
If you or someone you know experiences these, it's a RED FLAG:

They message you privately & quickly become "too friendly."
They ask personal questions or bring up inappropriate topics.
They try to isolate you from friends & family.
They pressure you to send photos, meet up, or keep secrets.
They get angry, guilt-trip, or threaten you if you don't comply.
They ask you to move the conversation outside of the app (e.g., from Instagram to Snapchat, WhatsApp, or another platform **to avoid being tracked**).

Example: A girl starts talking to a guy online. He says, *"Don't tell your parents about me, they wouldn't understand."* He then asks her to send *"just one"* private photo, promising he won't show anyone—but later, he **demands more or threatens to leak it.**

Tip: If someone is **rushing intimacy** or asking for secrecy, **it's a major red flag.**

---

3. What to Do if You or Someone You Know is Being Groomed
If You Suspect Grooming:

Trust your instincts—if something feels off, it probably is.
Stop responding & block the person immediately.
Save all messages, screenshots, and evidence.

Report them to the platform & authorities (Cybercrime Units, Child Protection Agencies).
Tell a trusted adult, parent, teacher, or friend.

Example: A girl realizes her **"online boyfriend"** is pressuring her for explicit photos. Instead of giving in, she **blocks him, tells her parents, and reports the account to Instagram and local authorities.**

If You See a Friend in a Suspicious Online Relationship:

Talk to them privately—express concern for their safety.
Encourage them to stop communicating & report the predator.
Remind them that real love and friendship don't involve secrecy, control, or pressure.
Help them gather evidence & seek help from an adult or authority.

Example: A girl notices her best friend is constantly messaging an **older guy online**. When she brings it up, her friend says, *"You wouldn't understand, he really cares about me."* Instead of ignoring it, she **shares articles about online grooming and encourages her friend to talk to a counselor.**

Tip: Predators manipulate victims into believing they're in control. Friends and family **should approach them with understanding, not judgment.**

Conclusion: Stay Aware, Stay Safe
Predators exploit vulnerability, trust, and secrecy to manipulate victims.
Recognizing grooming tactics, watching for red flags, and taking action can protect you and others.

Key Takeaways:

✔ Predators gain trust before exploiting victims—stay cautious.
✔ Online relationships should never involve secrecy, pressure, or manipulation.
✔ If something feels wrong, report it and seek help immediately.

Digital Safety Checklist

Keep personal details private online.
Avoid accepting friend requests from strangers.
If someone makes you uncomfortable, **block & report them.**
Never send private photos or engage in secretive relationships.
If a friend is in a dangerous online relationship, **support them and encourage them to seek help.**

Chapter 14: The Role of Schools & Parents in Social Media Safety

Building a Safe Digital Environment – Parents, Schools & Reporting Cyber Issues

---

Introduction

Parents and schools play a **crucial role** in protecting young girls from online dangers. However, **strict control or privacy invasion** can often lead to secrecy instead of safety. Instead of enforcing harsh restrictions, the focus should be on **guiding, educating, and empowering** children to navigate the digital world responsibly.

This chapter will cover:
- ✔ **How parents can guide & protect without invading privacy**
- ✔ **Cyber safety education & awareness programs in schools**
- ✔ **How to report cyber issues to school authorities**

---

1. How Parents Can Guide & Protect Without Invading Privacy

Many teenagers **reject strict parental control** because they see it as an invasion of their privacy. However, parents can still ensure their child's safety without resorting to excessive monitoring.

DO: Healthy Ways to Keep Your Child Safe Online

✔ **Build trust & open communication** – Encourage your child to talk about their online experiences.

✔ **Teach digital safety skills** – Instead of controlling, help them **recognize online risks** themselves.

✔ **Set up basic parental controls** – Use content filters, but **don't spy on their personal messages**.

✔ **Encourage critical thinking** – Ask, *"Would you say this in person?"* to help them reflect on their online behavior.

✔ **Lead by example** – Parents should also **practice online safety** by avoiding oversharing.

Example: Instead of secretly reading his daughter's messages, a father **has weekly discussions** about online safety, asking: *"What would you do if a stranger messaged you?"*

This approach **builds awareness instead of fear** and helps his daughter develop online safety skills.

DON'T: Over-Monitoring & Invading Privacy

Reading private messages & social media DMs without consent. Forcing children to give passwords (unless absolutely necessary). Banning social media completely (**leads to secrecy, not safety**). Using tracking apps **without discussing it first**.

Example: A mother **constantly checks** her teenage daughter's phone without telling her. The daughter starts **hiding things and using secret accounts**. Instead, the mother could have used **an open and honest approach** to discuss online safety.

Tip: Children are more likely to share their online experiences when they feel trusted and supported.

---

2. Cyber Safety Education & Awareness Programs in Schools

Schools have a **responsibility** to teach students about:
Online risks and how to **avoid scams, phishing, and fake accounts.**
Cyberbullying and online harassment—recognizing & responding.
Strong passwords & privacy settings—protecting personal information.
Online grooming & manipulation tactics—how predators target victims.
The impact of social media on mental health & self-esteem.
Reporting cyber threats & seeking help when in danger.

Example: A school **conducts monthly cyber safety workshops** where students learn how to **block, report, and recognize online scams**.

Best Practices for Schools

✔ Cyber safety **should be part of the school curriculum**.
✔ Schools should **organize workshops** & real-life case studies on online safety.
✔ Teachers should be **trained to recognize signs of online abuse**.
✔ Schools should provide **anonymous reporting systems** for students.

Example: A school introduces **an anonymous online reporting system** where students can report cyberbullying without fear of retaliation.

Tip: Cyber safety education should not be a one-time lesson—it must be an ongoing discussion.

3. How to Report Cyber Issues to School Authorities

Many students **experience cyberbullying, blackmail, or harassment** but **don't know how or where to report it**.

When Should You Report to the School?

✔ If you are **being cyberbullied** by classmates.
✔ If you see **harmful rumors, threats, or fake accounts** targeting students.
✔ If someone is **pressuring students for explicit content**.
✔ If students are **engaging in dangerous online challenges**.

Example: A student **sees a classmate being harassed** in a school group chat. She **takes screenshots** and **reports it to the school counselor.**

Steps to Report Cyber Issues at School

Step 1: Gather evidence (screenshots, messages, URLs).
Step 2: Report the issue to a **teacher, counselor, or school administrator.**
Step 3: If **no action is taken**, escalate the issue to the **school board** or **local authorities.**
Step 4: If the issue involves **threats, harassment, or blackmail, contact the police or cybercrime units.**

Example: A girl is blackmailed by a **senior student** at her school. She reports it to a teacher, but **no action is taken**. She then **informs the school principal and her parents, who escalate the issue to authorities.**

Tip: If your school does not take cyber safety seriously, push for stronger policies and accountability.

Conclusion: A Team Effort for a Safer Digital World
Parents must balance safety & privacy while guiding children.
Schools must provide cyber safety education & awareness programs.
Students should know when & how to report cyber issues.

Key Takeaways:

✔ **Open communication builds trust—spying does not.**
✔ **Cyber safety should be a mandatory part of education.**
✔ **Reporting cyber threats can prevent harm to others.**

Beyond Personal Safety: The Role of Online Activism & Advocacy
Social media is also a platform for **activism and social change—** but engaging in activism **safely** is crucial.

The Impact of Online Activism

Movements like #MeToo & #SayNoToHarassment have empowered women to **speak up** about abuse.
Social media **raises awareness about gender equality, harassment, and human rights**.

Example: A young girl shares her story about online harassment using **#SayNoToHarassment**, inspiring others to come forward.

How to Support Women's Rights While Staying Safe

✔ **Use anonymous accounts** if speaking about sensitive topics.
✔ **Be mindful of online backlash & trolls**—don't engage with toxic users.
✔ **Avoid sharing personal locations** or real-time updates in activism posts.
✔ **Know when to report & block** abusive users.

The Rise of Online Misogyny & How to Fight Back Safely

Women and girls often face **harassment, threats, and hate speech** online.
Misogynistic groups spread **toxic narratives and victim-blaming**.

How to Respond:
✔ **Call out harmful content, but prioritize your safety.**
✔ **Use report features & encourage others to do the same.**
✔ **Educate people about online harassment laws & consequences.**
✔ **Support platforms that take a stand against misogyny.**

Example: A student **witnesses sexist comments** in an online school forum. Instead of ignoring it, she **reports the comments & educates her peers on online respect**.

Tip: Online activism is powerful, but safety should always come first.

Chapter 15: Digital Feminism & Women's Rights in Cyberspace

Online Activism & Women's Rights – Staying Safe While Taking a Stand

Introduction

Social media has become a **powerful tool for activism**, allowing women to **speak out** against harassment, demand justice, and push for gender equality. However, activism also comes with risks—**harassment, doxxing, and cyber-attacks**.

This chapter will cover:
✔ **The impact of online activism** (#MeToo, #SayNoToHarassment, etc.)
✔ **How to support women's rights while staying safe online**
✔ **The rise of online misogyny & how to fight back safely**

---

1. The Impact of Online Activism (#MeToo, #SayNoToHarassment & More)

How Has Online Activism Changed the Fight for Women's Rights?

In the past, women had **limited platforms** to raise their voices. Today, social media movements have:

✔ **Exposed harassment & abuse** (#MeToo, #SayNoToHarassment)
✔ **Held powerful figures accountable** (celebrities, politicians, corporations)
✔ **Created global awareness** about women's rights issues
✔ **Connected survivors & activists** worldwide

Example:
The **#MeToo movement** started as a **small hashtag** and grew into a **global movement**, leading to **real-world consequences**—high-profile individuals faced legal action, and workplace policies changed.

Notable Online Activism Movements

#MeToo – Empowered survivors to share stories of **sexual harassment & assault**.
#SayNoToHarassment – Raised awareness about **everyday**

harassment women face.

#TimesUp – Advocated for **workplace equality & legal action against harassers**.

#GirlsNotObjects – Fought against the **sexualization of women in media**.

#DigitalSafetyForWomen – Educated women on **staying safe online**.

Example:
In 2019, a young woman in **India** shared her **harassment experience** at work under **#MeTooIndia**. Her post **went viral**, leading to an **official investigation** against the accused.

---

2. How to Support Women's Rights While Staying Safe Online

Risks of Online Activism

Trolling & Harassment – Activists often receive **hate messages & threats**.

Doxxing (Exposure of Personal Information) – Attackers may **leak private details**.

Cyber Attacks – Hackers may target **outspoken women**.

False Reporting & Account Suspension – Trolls may **mass-report** an activist's account.

Example:
A woman shares her **harassment experience**, and **online trolls flood her account** with **threats & abuse**.

Safety Tips for Online Activists

✔ **Use Strong Privacy Settings**
Keep personal details (phone number, location, workplace) **private**.
Set social media accounts to **private or restricted mode** when

necessary.

Use **two-factor authentication** to prevent hacking.

✔ Think Before You Share Personal Stories
Consider using an **alias or anonymous account** if sharing a sensitive story.
Avoid posting **exact locations, workplaces, or identifiable details**.

✔ Prepare for Backlash
Expect **criticism & trolling** – but **don't engage with abusers**.
Have a **support system** (trusted friends, family, legal support) ready.

✔ Use Anonymous Reporting & Secure Messaging
If exposing **powerful figures**, use **secure email services** (*ProtonMail, Tutanota*).
Use **encrypted messaging apps** (*Signal, Telegram*) for sensitive discussions.

Example:
A journalist covering **online harassment** keeps her social media **private**, uses a **work alias**, and shares her findings on **secure platforms** to **avoid doxxing**.

The Growing Threat of Online Misogyny

Many activists **face coordinated attacks** from misogynistic groups, who:

Send rape & death threats to silence women.
Create fake accounts to spread **misinformation**.
Doxx and harass outspoken activists.
Organize online hate campaigns.

Example:
A well-known feminist **speaks out** against online harassment. Within hours, **thousands of trolls flood her social media** with **threats, insults, and false accusations**.

How to Fight Back Against Online Misogyny (Safely)

✔ **Block & Report Abusers**
Don't engage—**block, mute, and report** trolls immediately. Platforms like **Twitter, Instagram, and Facebook** allow **mass reporting** of abusive accounts.

✔ **Keep Digital Evidence**
Take **screenshots** of threats & harassment for **legal action**. Report **serious threats** to **the police or cybercrime authorities**.

✔ **Call Out Misogyny Without Risking Yourself**
Use **group advocacy** – *Collective voices are harder to silence than individuals.*
Support **online communities** that focus on **women's rights & online safety**.

✔ **Use Technology to Stay Safe**
Google yourself to check if personal info is **publicly available**. Use **privacy protection tools** (*Blur, DeleteMe*) to **remove personal data** from the internet.

Example:
A woman **facing online threats** contacts an **anti-harassment legal group** for guidance. She **saves all messages**, reports threats to **authorities**, and **removes her private info** from public databases.

Conclusion: A Stronger, Safer Digital Future for Women
Online activism has given women a powerful voice, but it also comes with risks. By using privacy strategies, security tools, and

strong communities, women can continue to **fight for their rights while staying safe online**.

Key Takeaways:

✔ **Online activism has led to real-world change**—but also **risks harassment**.
✔ **Activists should use privacy settings, secure communication & strong passwords**.
✔ **The best way to fight misogyny is through collective action & smart digital safety**.

Additional Resources

Cyber Safety Organizations: Digital Rights Foundation, Take Back the Tech, Cyber Civil Rights Initiative
Secure Communication Tools: ProtonMail, Signal, Tor Browser
Reporting Cyber Harassment: Facebook & Twitter Report Centers, National Cybercrime Portals

Introduction

In today's digital world, **social media can make or break career opportunities**. Employers, clients, and recruiters often check **social media profiles** before hiring or collaborating. A single **controversial post, inappropriate comment, or online scandal** can **destroy job prospects or professional reputations**.

This chapter will cover:

✔ **How past social media activity can impact job opportunities**
✔ **Building a professional online presence**
✔ **Avoiding exploitation as an influencer or content creator**

1. How Past Social Media Activity Can Impact Job Opportunities

Why Employers Check Social Media Before Hiring

Recruiters and employers review **social media profiles** to evaluate a candidate's:

✔ **Professionalism** – Are they **mature, responsible, and respectful** online?
✔ **Cultural Fit** – Do their **values and interests align** with the company?
✔ **Red Flags** – Any **offensive, inappropriate, or illegal behavior**?

Example:
A candidate for a **marketing position** had **excellent qualifications**, but recruiters found **old offensive tweets** from years ago. As a result, she **lost the job opportunity**.

Social Media Red Flags That Can Cost You a Job

Offensive, racist, sexist, or discriminatory posts.
Public complaints about previous employers or colleagues.
Sharing confidential work-related information.
Unprofessional photos (drunken behavior, explicit content, etc.).
Engaging in online fights, arguments, or cyberbullying.

Example:
A teacher **applicant** was **denied a job** after the school board found **party photos with inappropriate behavior** on her Instagram.

How to Clean Up Your Social Media Before Job Hunting

✔ **Google Yourself** – Search your name and see what appears.
✔ **Delete or make private old posts** that could be controversial.
✔ **Review privacy settings** – Restrict past posts to **"Friends Only."**
✔ **Use separate accounts** for personal and professional life.
✔ **Avoid engaging in public online conflicts** or heated debates.

Example:
A job seeker **deleted old embarrassing tweets**, updated her **LinkedIn with professional achievements**, and made her **personal Instagram private**. Soon after, she **secured a top job in her field**.

2. Building a Professional Online Presence
Social media is **not just a risk**—it is also an **opportunity** to showcase **skills, knowledge, and personal branding**.

Steps to Build a Strong & Positive Online Presence

✔ **Optimize LinkedIn** – Keep your **resume updated**, share **industry insights**, and **connect with professionals**.
✔ **Showcase Achievements** – Post about **certifications, projects, and career milestones**.
✔ **Engage in Industry Conversations** – Comment on **relevant topics** on LinkedIn or Twitter.
✔ **Avoid Posting Controversial Topics** – *Politics, religion, and divisive issues can create problems.*
✔ **Use Professional Profile Pictures** – Avoid **blurry, low-quality, or inappropriate images**.

Example:
A college graduate **started sharing blog posts** about **marketing trends** on **LinkedIn**. A company saw her work and **offered her a job**.

The Power of Networking Online

✔ **Join industry-specific groups** on **LinkedIn & Facebook**.
✔ **Attend virtual conferences & webinars**.
✔ **Engage with posts** by industry leaders & professionals.
✔ **Post valuable content** to position yourself as a **knowledgeable professional**.

Example:
A **software engineer** actively participated in **LinkedIn discussions** about AI. A **recruiter noticed his expertise** and **offered him a job**.

---

3. Avoiding Exploitation as an Influencer or Content Creator

Social media **influencers and content creators** can earn income through **sponsorships, brand deals, and content monetization**.

However, the industry also has **many risks**, including **exploitation, scams, and mental burnout**.

Dangers in the Influencer Industry

Unpaid Brand Collaborations – Some brands take advantage of influencers by offering **"exposure" instead of payment**.
Scams & Fake Contracts – Fraudulent companies trick influencers into **signing bad deals**.
Privacy Invasion – Stalkers and **online threats** can become real dangers.
Mental Health Issues – The pressure to constantly post, look perfect, and get likes can cause **anxiety & burnout**.

Example:
A **young influencer** was promised **free products and a brand partnership** but **never got paid**. The company **disappeared after using her content**.

How to Protect Yourself as an Influencer

✔ **Read contracts carefully** – Always clarify **payment terms before signing**.
✔ **Charge for your work** – *Exposure doesn't pay bills; ask for fair compensation.*
✔ **Protect personal information** – Avoid sharing **home addresses or private details**.
✔ **Set boundaries** – Take **breaks from social media** to prevent burnout.
✔ **Be selective with brands** – Work only with **trustworthy companies**.

Example:
A **beauty influencer** only **accepts paid collaborations** with

reputable brands and keeps **business & personal accounts separate** for safety.

Conclusion: Social Media as a Career Tool – Use It Wisely

Your **online presence** can either **help or hurt your future**. By **cleaning up past content, building a professional image, and protecting yourself from exploitation**, you can **use social media to create opportunities instead of risks**.

Key Takeaways:

✔ **Employers check social media before hiring**—always **keep it professional**.
✔ **A positive online image** helps build **credibility & career opportunities**.
✔ **Influencers must protect themselves** from **scams, privacy threats & mental burnout**.

Additional Resources

Professional Networking Platforms: LinkedIn, AngelList, Glassdoor
Privacy Tools: Blur, DeleteMe, Privacy Badger
Influencer Legal Protection: CreatorIQ, Influencer Marketing Hub

Chapter 17.Protecting Yourself Online

Introduction

The internet is full of risks, from **hackers stealing personal data** to **spyware tracking online activities**. Many cybercriminals **target girls and women specifically**, using **malware, phishing, and tracking tools** to exploit them.

This chapter will cover:
✔ **Using VPNs, encrypted messaging apps & anonymous browsing**
✔ **Understanding malware, spyware & online tracking**
✔ **How hackers target girls & how to stay safe**

---

1 Using VPNs, Encrypted Messaging Apps & Anonymous Browsing

What is a VPN & Why Do You Need One?

A **VPN (Virtual Private Network)** hides your IP address and encrypts your internet activity, making it difficult for hackers, stalkers, or cybercriminals to track you.

Benefits of Using a VPN:
Hides your location & IP address – Prevents tracking.
Secures public Wi-Fi use – Protects from hackers in coffee shops, airports, etc.
Prevents government or ISP surveillance – Keeps your browsing private.

Best VPNs for Privacy:
NordVPN – Strong encryption, no-logs policy.
ExpressVPN – Fast speeds, reliable security.
ProtonVPN – Privacy-focused, free version available.

Encrypted Messaging Apps: Keeping Conversations Private

Many social media apps **collect and store messages**, making private chats **vulnerable to leaks or hacking**.

Use These Secure Messaging Apps:
Signal – End-to-end encryption, no data collection.
Telegram (Secret Chats) – Self-deleting messages, encryption.
WhatsApp – Encrypted, but owned by Meta (less private).

Example: A girl experiencing cyberstalking **switches to Signal** to keep her conversations private and prevent tracking.

Anonymous Browsing: How to Hide Your Online Activities

Some websites and social media platforms **track every move you make** online. Anonymous browsing helps keep **your searches, locations, and activities hidden**.

Best Tools for Anonymous Browsing:
Brave Browser – Blocks ads & trackers automatically.
DuckDuckGo Search Engine – Doesn't save search history.
Tor Browser – Provides complete anonymity, but may slow browsing.

Example: A journalist covering sensitive topics **uses the Tor browser and a VPN** to protect her identity.

---

2 Understanding Malware, Spyware & Online Tracking
What is Malware & How Does It Infect Devices?

Malware (malicious software) includes viruses, spyware, and ransomware that hackers use to:
Steal passwords & financial info.
Track keystrokes (what you type).

Access your webcam & microphone.
Lock files & demand ransom payments.

Example: A girl downloads a free beauty filter app that secretly contains spyware. It **steals her photos and messages** without her knowledge.

How to Protect Yourself from Malware:
Avoid downloading unknown apps or files.
Use trusted antivirus software (Norton, Bitdefender, Avast).
Never click on suspicious links in emails or messages.

How Spyware & Stalkers Track You Online

Spyware is software that secretly monitors and collects your private information.
Hackers, ex-partners, and even strangers **may install spyware** on phones to track girls.

Example: A woman's ex-boyfriend secretly installs a spyware app on her phone, tracking her calls, messages, and GPS location.

How to Detect & Remove Spyware:
Check for unusual apps in your phone settings.
Use anti-spyware tools like Malwarebytes or Certo Mobile Security.
Reset your device if you suspect spyware.

Online Tracking: How Companies & Hackers Collect Data

Many websites and social media apps **track user behavior** to collect:
Location data
Search history
Access to your camera & microphone

How to Stop Online Tracking:
Turn off location services on social media apps.
Use browser extensions like Privacy Badger to block trackers.
Regularly delete cookies & browsing history.

Example: A social media influencer notices **ads for products she only discussed privately**—this happens because her microphone permissions were ON.

---

3 How Hackers Target Girls & How to Stay Safe
Common Hacking Techniques Used Against Girls

Phishing Emails & Messages – Fake links that steal passwords.
Fake Job Offers & Modeling Scams – Hackers pretend to offer jobs to steal data.
Social Engineering Tricks – Hackers **pretend to be friends, celebrities, or even companies** to gain trust.
Password Guessing – Weak passwords make hacking easy.

Example: A girl receives a **fake message pretending to be from Instagram Support**, asking her to verify her account. She **clicks the link and loses access** to

1. Using VPNs, Encrypted Messaging Apps & Anonymous Browsing

This section will cover the essential tools and methods for maintaining online privacy and security.

1.1 Virtual Private Networks (VPNs)

- **What is a VPN?**

  - How VPNs work: encrypting internet traffic, hiding IP addresses, and securing public Wi-Fi usage.

  - The difference between free and paid VPNs.

  - How VPNs protect against tracking and ISP monitoring.

- ## How to Choose a Good VPN

  - Features to look for: no-logs policy, strong encryption, kill switch, speed, and global server network.

  - Recommended VPN providers and how to set them up.

- ## VPN Limitations

  - Does a VPN make you completely anonymous?

  - How some websites detect and block VPN usage.

  - When to combine a VPN with other privacy tools.

1.2 Encrypted Messaging Apps

- ## Why Encryption Matters

  - How end-to-end encryption (E2EE) works.

  - Difference between client-side and server-side encryption.

- ## Best Encrypted Messaging Apps

  - **Signal** – Open-source, strong encryption, no data collection.

  - **Telegram** – Optional encryption, secret chats, self-destructing messages.

  - **WhatsApp** – E2EE but owned by Meta (privacy concerns).

- ## How to Stay Secure While Messaging

  - Verifying encryption keys.

  - Avoiding screenshots and backups.

  - Using disappearing messages and self-destructing media.

1.3 Anonymous Browsing

- ## How Websites Track You

  - Cookies, fingerprinting, IP logging, and tracking scripts.

  - How social media and search engines collect data.

- **How to Browse Anonymously**

  - **Tor Browser** – Routing traffic through multiple nodes.

  - **Brave & Firefox** – Privacy-focused browsers with tracking protection.

  - **DuckDuckGo & Startpage** – Search engines that don't track users.

- **Other Privacy Tools**

  - Ad blockers (uBlock Origin, Privacy Badger).

  - Browser extensions for script blocking.

  - Using disposable email addresses.

---

2. Understanding Malware, Spyware & Online Tracking

This section will explain various cybersecurity threats and how to protect against them.

2.1 Malware

- **Types of Malware**

  - Viruses, Trojans, Worms, Ransomware, and Rootkits.

  - How they spread through emails, downloads, and malicious links.

- **How to Protect Against Malware**

  - Keeping software and operating systems updated.

  - Using strong antivirus software.

  - Avoiding suspicious links and downloads.

2.2 Spyware & Stalkerware

- **What is Spyware?**

  - Spyware collects data without user knowledge.

- Keyloggers, screen capture software, and microphone access.

- ## Stalkerware: A Special Threat

  - Abusers use stalkerware to track victims.

  - Detect and remove stalkerware from your phone or computer.

- ## Companies Track You Online

  - Google, Facebook, and data brokers.

  - The risks of personalized ads and behavioral profiling.

- ## How to Minimize Tracking

  - Using privacy-focused browsers and search engines.

  - Turning off ad personalization in Google and social media settings.

  - Clearing cookies and cache regularly.

---

3. How Hackers Target Girls & How to Stay Safe

This section will focus on digital threats specifically affecting women and girls, including online harassment, doxxing, and catfishing.

- ## Online Harassment & Cyberbullying

  - Tactics used by harassers: trolling, hate speech, mass reporting.

  - Report and block harassers on different platforms.

- ## Doxxing & Information Exposure

  - Personal data is leaked or sold.

  - Steps to remove personal data from the internet.

- **Catfishing & Romance Scams**

  - Scammers pretend to be someone they're not.

  - Warning signs of a romance scammer.

- **Social Media Privacy Settings**

  - Locking down accounts on Facebook, Instagram, and Twitter.

  - Controlling who can see your posts and personal information.

- **Secure Passwords & Multi-Factor Authentication (MFA)**

  - Using password managers.

  - Enabling MFA for social media, email, and banking apps.

- **Protecting Against Sextortion & Blackmail**

  - Recognizing signs of manipulation.

  - What to do if someone threatens to leak your private photos.

  - Legal protections and reporting options.

- **Where to Get Help**

  - Cyber harassment helplines.

  - Legal actions for online threats.

Cyber Harassment Helplines & Legal Support

- **Cybersecurity and Infrastructure Security Agency (CISA)** – Provides cybersecurity resources and guidance.

    o Contact: 1-888-282-0870 | Email: central@cisa.dhs.gov

- **Emergency Situations:** Call **911** for immediate threats.

- **Action Fraud** – The UK's national reporting center for fraud and cybercrime.

    - Contact: 0300 123 2040 (Monday–Friday, 8 AM–8 PM)

- **National Crime Agency (NCA)** – For non-urgent cybercrimes, contact local police by calling **101**.

- **National Cyber Security Centre (NCSC)** – Provides guidance on cybersecurity threats.

    - Website: www.ncsc.gov.uk

- **Immediate Threats:** Call **999** for urgent situations.

- **National Cyber Crime Helpline:** Dial **1930** for reporting cybercrimes, including online harassment and financial fraud.

- **National Women Helpline:** Call **181** for women's safety-related issues.

- **Delhi Commission for Women:** Contact **+91-11-23379181** or **181** for assistance.

- **Child Helpline:** Dial **1098** for child-related concerns.

- **Online Reporting Portal:** Report cybercrimes at cybercrime.gov.in.

Legal Actions for Online Threats

India has established laws to combat cyber harassment:

- **Information Technology (IT) Act, 2000** – Addresses cybercrimes; Section 66D deals with online fraud and impersonation.

- **Indian Penal Code (IPC)** – Section 354A addresses sexual harassment, punishable by up to three years in prison.

Steps to Take

1. **Report to Local Police** – File a First Information Report (FIR) at your nearest police station.

2. **Use the National Cyber Crime Reporting Portal** – Submit complaints online.

3. **Seek Legal Counsel** – Consult cyber law professionals for advice.

4. **Preserve Evidence** – Save screenshots, emails, and chat logs to support your case.

Signs of Social Media Dependency & How to Break Free

Recognizing Social Media Addiction

- **Checking notifications constantly** – Feeling the urge to check messages, likes, or comments even during conversations, meals, or work.

- **Anxiety when offline** – Feeling restless, anxious, or "disconnected" when not using social media.

- **Using social media as an emotional escape** – Turning to social media to relieve stress, boredom, or sadness instead of dealing with emotions directly.

- **Comparing yourself to others** – Feeling dissatisfied with life due to curated highlight reels on social media.

- **Neglecting real-life relationships** – Spending more time online than with friends or family.

- **Disrupted sleep patterns** – Scrolling late at night and feeling tired during the day.

The Psychological Tricks That Keep You Hooked

- **Endless scrolling and autoplay** – Platforms continuously load new content to keep users engaged.

- **Social validation (likes, comments, shares)** – Dopamine spikes from online approval create addiction-like behavior.

- **Fear of Missing Out (FOMO)** – Anxiety about missing important updates, trends, or events.

- **Push notifications and urgency tactics** – Apps use "urgent" notifications to trigger immediate engagement.

- **Set daily time limits** – Use screen time tracking apps to monitor usage and set restrictions.

- **Disable unnecessary notifications** – Reduce distractions by turning off non-essential alerts.

- **Create "no-phone" zones** – Keep devices out of bedrooms, dining tables, and social gatherings.

- **Replace screen time with real-world activities** – Engage in hobbies, exercise, and face-to-face interactions.

- **Unfollow toxic accounts** – Curate a healthier digital space by removing negative or addictive content.

Final Thoughts

Balancing digital life with real-world interactions is essential for mental well-being. Social media can be a useful tool, but excessive use leads to addiction, stress, and reduced productivity. By setting boundaries and making conscious choices, you can take back control and use technology in a way that benefits your life instead of consuming it.

Building a Safer Digital Culture

Online spaces should be safe for everyone, yet cyber harassment, doxxing, and online abuse disproportionately affect women and marginalized groups. Boys and men have a crucial role in shaping a respectful digital culture by promoting ethical behavior, challenging toxicity, and becoming allies in online safety.

This chapter will cover: ✔ Why men play a role in online safety
✔ Ways to be an ally in digital spaces
✔ Educating boys about respectful online behavior
✔ Addressing toxic masculinity & online harassment
✔ How to build a positive digital environment

---

1. Why Men Have a Role in Online Safety
Understanding the Problem

- Women and marginalized groups experience higher rates of cyberstalking, threats, and harassment.

- Studies show that most online harassment is perpetrated by men, yet many are unaware of its impact.

- Silence equals complicity—staying silent when witnessing harassment normalizes the behavior.

Why Male Allies Matter

- When men speak out against harassment, they influence digital culture and encourage change.

- Men are less likely to face backlash for calling out toxic behavior compared to women.

- Being an ally means supporting women, amplifying their voices, and challenging harmful online norms.

Call Out Misogynistic or Harassing Behavior

- Speak up against sexist jokes, degrading comments, and online harassment.

- Example: "That comment is inappropriate—let's keep the discussion respectful."

Support Women & Marginalized Groups Online

- Offer public or private support to those facing harassment.

- Report abusive accounts instead of ignoring them.

- Follow and promote content creators who encourage respectful discourse.

Create Inclusive & Respectful Online Communities

- If you manage online spaces (forums, Discord servers, gaming groups), establish strict anti-harassment policies.

- Encourage discussions on gender respect, digital ethics, and online safety.

The Importance of Early Digital Education

- Boys are exposed to toxic online behavior through gaming, social media, and forums at a young age.

109

- Many grow up believing that sexist jokes, harassment, and aggressive behavior online are acceptable.

- Digital respect should be taught just like real-world respect.

Teaching Boys About Online Respect & Consent

Online Harassment & Its Consequences

- Educate boys on what constitutes harassment, threats, revenge porn, and cyberstalking.

- Explain how these actions harm real people and may have legal consequences.

Respecting Boundaries & Consent Online

- Teach boys not to send unsolicited messages, inappropriate images, or pressure someone online.

- Reinforce that "No" means "No," even in digital interactions.

- Encourage asking for permission before sharing someone's photos or personal information.

Recognizing & Rejecting Toxic Influences

- Many online spaces promote misogyny, incel culture, and gender-based hate.

- Teach boys to question influencers who encourage aggressive masculinity or belittle women.

- Encourage critical thinking about online content and peer groups.

How Parents, Schools, & Role Models Can Help

- Parents should start conversations about respectful online behavior early.

- Schools should integrate digital ethics into online safety lessons.

- Male role models can set positive examples through their online interactions.

4. Addressing Toxic Masculinity & Online Harassment
How Toxic Masculinity Fuels Online Abuse

What is Toxic Masculinity?
Toxic masculinity promotes harmful beliefs such as:

- Men must assert dominance, especially over women.

- Expressing emotions is a sign of weakness.

- Sexual conquest and aggression define masculinity.

These beliefs contribute to misogyny, sexual harassment, and online abuse.

How It Manifests in Online Spaces
- **Trolling & Harassment** – Some men resort to bullying to assert dominance.

- **Revenge Porn & Non-Consensual Image Sharing** – Treating women's bodies as commodities fuels image-based abuse.

- **Incels & Anti-Feminist Groups** – Radical online communities promote gender-based resentment and violence.

Breaking the Cycle of Online Misogyny

Encouraging Emotional Intelligence
- Teach boys that empathy, kindness, and vulnerability are strengths.

111

- Promote healthy emotional coping mechanisms instead of aggression.

Disrupting Harmful Online Spaces

- Parents, teachers, and mentors should engage in conversations about the online spaces boys frequent.

- Platforms should actively moderate and remove misogynistic communities that incite violence.

Holding Platforms Accountable

- Tech companies must take responsibility for moderating abusive behavior.

- Governments should implement stricter regulations on cyber harassment and hate speech.

Conclusion: Shaping a Safer Digital Future

A safer online culture requires education, accountability, and action. By challenging toxic behaviors, educating boys, and supporting victims, we can create a digital space that promotes respect, equality, and safety for everyone.

AI, Misinformation & Online Manipulation

How AI-Generated Media Is Used for Manipulation
What Is AI-Generated Media?

- AI-generated media refers to text, images, videos, and audio created by artificial intelligence using deep learning models.

- Examples include:

  - **Deepfake videos** – AI-generated videos that replace a person's face or voice.

  - **AI-written news articles** – Fake news or propaganda created by AI-powered bots.

  - **Synthetic voice cloning** – AI-generated voices that mimic real people.

  - **AI-generated images & social media personas** – Fake profiles or misleading images created using AI.

How AI Is Used for Online Manipulation

Political Propaganda & Election Influence
- AI is used to create fake political speeches, altered videos, and misleading images to manipulate public opinion.

- Automated bot networks spread false narratives across social media.

Financial & Stock Market Manipulation
- AI-generated fake news can influence stock prices and cause market disruptions.

- Fake CEO announcements or deepfake interviews can mislead investors.

Scams & Identity Fraud

- AI-generated voice deepfakes are used for impersonation scams (e.g., fake emergency calls from "relatives" asking for money).

- Criminals use deepfake job interviews to commit fraud.

Misinformation in Journalism & Social Media

- AI-generated fake news articles are designed to look real, spreading false information.

- AI-generated social media influencers (like XY) blur the lines between reality and fiction.

Detecting Fake News, Misinformation & Deepfakes

How to Identify Fake News & AI-Generated Misinformation

Check the Source

- Look for official sources, domain names, and credibility of the website.

- Be wary of new, unknown news sites without a track record.

Analyze the Writing Style

- AI-generated articles often lack human nuance, repeat phrases, and feel overly structured.

- Watch out for clickbait headlines and emotionally charged language.

Fact-Check Claims Using Multiple Sources

- Cross-check news with trusted fact-checking websites (Snopes, FactCheck.org, Reuters).

- If only one website reports a major event, it's likely false or misleading.

Facial & Audio Clues

- Look for unnatural blinking, lip-sync mismatches, or distorted facial expressions.

- Audio deepfakes may have robotic tones, unnatural pauses, or inconsistent intonations.

Reverse Image Search

- Use Google Reverse Image Search or TinEye to check if an image is doctored or AI-generated.

Metadata Analysis

- Tools like FotoForensics or InVID can detect if an image/video has been manipulated.

Tools & Resources to Verify Online Content

Tools to Detect Misinformation

- **Snopes & FactCheck.org** – Verify viral claims and news articles.

- **Politifact** – Checks political statements and claims for accuracy.

- **NewsGuard** – Browser extension that rates news sources for reliability.

Tools to Detect Deepfakes & AI-Manipulated Media

- **Deepware Scanner** – Detects deepfake videos.

- **InVID & WeVerify** – Browser extensions for spotting fake images and videos.

- **Microsoft Video Authenticator** – AI tool to detect deepfake alterations.

- **Fake News Debunker by InVID** – Helps analyze suspect images and videos.

- **Hoaxy** – Tracks the spread of misinformation on social media.

- **Fotoforensics** – Analyzes digital images for manipulation.

Conclusion: Staying Informed & Fighting Digital Manipulation

- AI-generated media is becoming more sophisticated, making it harder to distinguish fact from fiction.

- Critical thinking, verification tools, and fact-checking habits are key to navigating the digital world safely.

- The future will require stronger digital literacy education to combat deepfake propaganda and online deception.

The Future of Digital Security

The Impact of AI, the Metaverse & Web3 on Digital Security

How AI Is Transforming Cybersecurity & Cyber Threats

- **AI as a Cybersecurity Tool**

  - AI-powered security systems can detect patterns of cyber threats and predict attacks before they happen.

  - Automated threat detection using machine learning and anomaly detection.

  - AI chatbots assist in fraud detection, security alerts, and user authentication.

- **AI in Cybercrime & Hacking**

  - Deepfake scams – AI-generated fake voices or videos used for fraud and misinformation.

  - AI-powered phishing attacks – Hackers use AI to create personalized phishing emails that mimic real users.

  - AI-generated malware – Malware that evolves and adapts to avoid detection.

Security Risks of the Metaverse

- **Identity Theft in Virtual Worlds**

  - Digital avatars and personal data in the Metaverse can be stolen or manipulated.

  - Biometric data (facial scans, fingerprints, eye tracking) could be used against users.

- **Cyber Harassment & Virtual Crimes**

  - Cases of virtual assault, cyberstalking, and harassment in Metaverse spaces.

  - Lack of clear laws on how to moderate and prosecute digital crimes in virtual environments.

- **Data Privacy Concerns**

  - The Metaverse collects massive amounts of personal data, from location tracking to user behaviors and interactions.

  - The risk of corporations and governments misusing this data for surveillance.

Web3 & Blockchain: A Double-Edged Sword for Security

- **Decentralization & Data Ownership**

  - Web3 gives users more control over their data through blockchain-based identity verification.

  - Personal data stored on decentralized networks reduces reliance on Big Tech.

- **Cybersecurity Challenges of Web3**

  - Smart contract vulnerabilities – Hackers exploit coding flaws in blockchain contracts.

  - Crypto scams & rug pulls – Web3 projects attract scams where investors lose millions.

  - Decentralized platforms lack regulation, making fraud easier to execute.

How Social Media Laws & Regulations Are Evolving

The Need for Stronger Social Media Regulations

- Governments worldwide are enacting new laws to hold tech platforms accountable for:

    - Spreading misinformation.

    - Privacy violations.

    - Enabling harassment and hate speech.

- Platforms like Facebook, Twitter, and TikTok are under pressure to increase moderation and improve data protection policies.

Recent & Upcoming Social Media Laws

- **Europe: The Digital Services Act (DSA) & GDPR Updates**

    - Requires platforms to take down illegal content faster.

    - Stricter rules on advertising and data collection.

- **United States: Section 230 Debate & AI Regulation**

    - Section 230 protects platforms from liability for user content, but new proposals seek to hold tech companies accountable for harmful content.

    - Possible AI regulations to monitor deepfake misuse and AI-generated misinformation.

- **China & Other Countries: Stricter Internet Censorship**

- China's Great Firewall restricts social media access.

- India, Russia, and other nations are enforcing data localization laws that require companies to store user data within national borders.

Future-Proofing Your Online Safety Skills

- **Use AI-Powered Security Tools**

- **Strengthen Your Digital Hygiene**

- **Navigate a More Decentralized Internet**

- **Stay Ahead of AI & Misinformation**

Conclusion: Securing Your Future in the Digital Age

Steps to Take If You're Being Harassed or Stalked Online

Recognizing Online Harassment & Stalking
Online harassment can include:

- **Cyberstalking** – Repeatedly sending messages, threats, or tracking your online activity.

- **Doxxing** – Sharing personal information (address, phone number) to intimidate you.

- **Revenge Porn & Non-Consensual Image Sharing** – Spreading private photos/videos without consent.

- **Impersonation & Fake Accounts** – Someone creating a fake profile pretending to be you.

- **Hate Speech & Trolling** – Offensive, sexist, or abusive messages targeting you.

Immediate Steps to Protect Yourself

- **Document Everything**

    - Take screenshots of messages, emails, posts, or threats.

    - Record timestamps and user profiles involved.

- **Secure Your Accounts**

    - Change passwords immediately & enable two-factor authentication (2FA).

    - Update privacy settings on social media (limit who can see your posts).

- Log out of all devices remotely if you suspect hacking.

- **Block & Report the Harasser**

  - Use the block feature on social media platforms, messaging apps, and email.

  - Report the account to the platform (Instagram, Facebook, Twitter, TikTok, etc.).

- **Warn Friends & Family**

  - Let close friends know if someone is impersonating you or spreading false information.

  - Ask them not to engage with the harasser to avoid escalation.

- **Avoid Engaging with the Harasser**

  - Don't respond or react emotionally. Harassers thrive on attention.

  - If threats escalate, contact law enforcement or a cybercrime unit.

How to Report Cybercrimes & Seek Legal Protection

When Should You Report Online Harassment to Authorities?

- If you feel physically unsafe or the harassment includes threats of harm.

- If your personal information, address, or intimate images have been leaked.

- If someone is blackmailing or extorting you online.

- If you suspect someone is stalking or tracking your online activity.

- **Social Media Platforms** – Report abusive content through in-app tools (Facebook, Instagram, Twitter, TikTok).

- **Cybercrime Units** – Many countries have dedicated cyber police or online safety departments.

- **Local Law Enforcement** – File a police report for harassment, stalking, or blackmail.

- **Internet Service Providers (ISP)** – If harassment involves email spam or hacking.

Understanding Cybercrime Laws in Different Countries

- **United States**: Report to the FBI's Internet Crime Complaint Center (IC3).

- **European Union**: Each country has cybercrime laws; report to Europol's Cybercrime Division.

- **United Kingdom**: Report to Action Fraud UK or the National Cyber Crime Unit (NCCU).

- **India**: File complaints at the National Cyber Crime Reporting Portal.

- **Australia**: Contact the eSafety Commissioner for online abuse cases.

Legal Protection Against Online Harassment

- **Restraining Orders & Digital Protection Orders** – Some courts issue orders to prevent online contact.

- **Revenge Porn Laws** – Many countries now have strict laws against sharing private images.

- **Anti-Doxxing Laws** – Some regions have laws criminalizing publicizing private information without consent.

- **Workplace & School Policies** – Universities and employers have policies to handle online harassment cases.

List of Global Helplines & Support Organizations

Cybercrime & Online Harassment Helplines

- **Cyber Civil Rights Initiative (CCRI)** – Helps victims of revenge porn & image-based abuse.

- **CyberSmile Foundation** – Offers support for cyberbullying victims.

- **STOPNCII.org** – Helps prevent non-consensual image leaks.

- **Revenge Porn Helpline (UK)** – Provides legal advice for victims.

Women's Safety & Domestic Violence Hotlines

- **RAINN (USA)** – Sexual assault support & online abuse resources.

- **Women's Aid (UK)** – Support for women facing online & offline harassment.

- **National Network to End Domestic Violence (NNEDV)** – Cybersecurity tips for abuse survivors.

Tech Platforms & Reporting Tools

- **Facebook & Instagram Safety Centers** – Guide for reporting and blocking users.

- **Google's "Remove Personal Information" Request** – Helps remove private data from search results.

- **Take It Down (Meta)** – Tool for removing private images from social media.

Conclusion: Taking Control of Your Digital Safety

- **Empowerment through knowledge** – Knowing your legal rights and how to respond is key.

- **Support networks** – No one should handle online harassment alone; seek help and report it.

- **Future digital security** – Stay proactive, use privacy tools, and educate others on online safety.

Why Cyber Hygiene Matters

- Practicing good cyber hygiene helps protect personal data, financial security, and online identity.

- Cyber threats such as hacking, phishing, and malware attacks can be prevented with simple daily habits.

Daily Cyber Hygiene Checklist

1. Use Strong & Unique Passwords

- Use a password manager to generate and store complex passwords.

- Avoid using the same password for multiple accounts.

- Change passwords periodically, especially for critical accounts (banking, email, social media).

2. Enable Two-Factor Authentication (2FA)

- Activate 2FA on all major accounts (email, banking, social media, cloud storage).

- Use authenticator apps instead of SMS for better security.

3. Beware of Phishing Scams

- Never click on suspicious links or download attachments from unknown sources.

- Verify sender details before responding to emails requesting personal information.

- Use email filtering tools to detect phishing attempts.

- Enable automatic updates for your operating system, apps, and antivirus software.

- Update web browsers and plugins regularly to fix security vulnerabilities.

5. Secure Your Internet Connection

- Use a strong Wi-Fi password and WPA3 encryption.

- Avoid using public Wi-Fi for sensitive transactions; use a VPN for added security.

6. Manage Your Social Media Privacy

- Adjust privacy settings to limit who can view your posts and personal information.

- Be cautious of friend requests and messages from unknown users.

- Regularly review and remove third-party apps connected to your accounts.

7. Regularly Back Up Important Data

- Use cloud storage or external drives to back up essential files.

- Set automatic backup schedules to prevent data loss from cyberattacks or hardware failure.

8. Use Antivirus & Anti-Malware Protection

- Install reputable antivirus software and keep it updated.

- Run regular system scans to detect and remove malware.

- Shop only on trusted websites (look for HTTPS in the URL).

- Use virtual or disposable credit cards for online purchases.

- Avoid saving payment information on websites.

- Always log out of shared or public devices.

- Enable automatic logouts for banking and sensitive applications.

- Google yourself periodically to see what personal information is publicly available.

- Remove outdated or sensitive information from online platforms.

- Look out for signs of account compromise (unexpected logins, password changes, or unknown transactions).

- Report suspicious activities to relevant platforms or authorities immediately.

Conclusion: Make Cyber Hygiene a Daily Habit

- Staying cyber-secure requires consistency and awareness.

- Implementing these habits will strengthen your digital safety and protect your online presence.

- Encourage family and friends to follow good cyber hygiene practices to create a safer online environment.

A Pledge for Responsible Online Behavior

Introduction

The internet and social media platforms provide endless opportunities for connection, learning, and entertainment. However, with these opportunities come risks such as cyberbullying, privacy invasions, misinformation, and online harassment. This Social Media Safety Contract serves as a personal commitment to responsible digital behavior, ensuring a safer and more positive online experience for everyone.

Social Media Safety Pledge

By signing this contract, I pledge to uphold the following responsible online behaviors:

1. Protecting My Privacy & Personal Information

- I will use strong, unique passwords and enable two-factor authentication (2FA) for my accounts.

- I will keep my personal information (address, phone number, school/workplace) private and avoid sharing sensitive details online.

- I will adjust my privacy settings to control who can see my posts, comments, and profile details.

- I will be cautious about sharing my location in real time.

2. Practicing Respectful & Kind Online Communication

- I will treat others with kindness and respect, avoiding hateful, offensive, or harmful language.

- I will not engage in cyberbullying, trolling, or spreading rumors.

- I will think before I post, ensuring my words and actions online reflect my values.

3. Recognizing & Avoiding Misinformation

- I will verify the authenticity of news and information before sharing it.

- I will use reliable fact-checking sources to confirm the credibility of online content.

- I will be skeptical of sensationalized headlines and manipulated media.

4. Being Cautious with Online Interactions

- I will be mindful of friend requests and messages from strangers.

- I will never share my passwords, login credentials, or private photos with anyone.

- I will avoid clicking on suspicious links or downloading unverified attachments.

- I will be aware of online scams and phishing attempts.

5. Managing My Digital Well-Being

- I will take breaks from social media to maintain a healthy balance between online and offline life.

- I will set screen time limits and be mindful of my mental and emotional well-being.

- I will unfollow or mute accounts that negatively impact my self-esteem or well-being.

- I will use social media to promote positivity and personal growth.

- I will report harmful or inappropriate content to platform moderators.

- I will support friends or peers who experience online harassment.

- I will seek help from trusted adults, professionals, or law enforcement if I feel threatened or unsafe online.

Agreement & Signature

By signing this contract, I acknowledge my responsibility in maintaining a safe, respectful, and informed presence online. I understand that my digital actions have real-world consequences and commit to using social media responsibly.

Signed: _____

Date: _____

Conclusion

A responsible approach to social media ensures a safer, healthier, and more positive online environment. This contract serves as a reminder to be mindful of our actions and contribute to a digital space that fosters respect, safety, and well-being.

Instructions:

Answer the following questions to assess your social media safety practices. Choose the option that best describes your online habits. At the end of the quiz, count your score and check the results to see how secure you are online.

Section 1: Account Security

1. Do you use a unique password for each of your social media accounts?

   - A) Yes, I use a password manager to store and create unique passwords. (3 points)

   - B) I reuse some passwords but try to make them strong. (2 points)

   - C) I use the same password for most accounts because it's easier to remember. (0 points)

- Have you enabled two-factor authentication (2FA) on your social media accounts?

   - A) Yes, for all my accounts. (3 points)

   - B) Only for my most important accounts. (2 points)

   - C) No, I find it inconvenient. (0 points)

- Do you regularly update your passwords?

   - A) Yes, every few months or whenever I suspect an issue. (3 points)

- B) I change them occasionally but not regularly. (2 points)

- C) No, I keep the same passwords for years. (0 points)

Section 2: Privacy & Data Protection

- Who can see your social media profiles and posts?

    - A) Only my approved friends and connections. (3 points)

    - B) Some posts are public, but most are private. (2 points)

    - C) My profile and posts are public for anyone to view. (0 points)

- Do you share personal information (full name, address, phone number, workplace, etc.) on social media?

    - A) No, I keep my personal information private. (3 points)

    - B) I share some details but avoid sensitive information. (2 points)

    - C) Yes, I share a lot of personal information online. (0 points)

- Do you review and update your privacy settings on social media?

    - A) Yes, I regularly check and adjust my settings. (3 points)

- B) Occasionally, but I don't always keep track. (2 points)

- C) No, I never bother with privacy settings. (0 points)

Section 3: Awareness of Online Threats

- How do you handle friend requests or messages from strangers on social media?

    - A) I ignore or block unknown requests/messages. (3 points)

    - B) I check their profiles before deciding. (2 points)

    - C) I accept most requests because I like connecting with new people. (0 points)

- Do you click on links sent via social media DMs or comments?

    - A) No, I verify links before clicking. (3 points)

    - B) Sometimes, if they seem trustworthy. (2 points)

    - C) Yes, I click on links without much thought. (0 points)

- Do you verify news or information before sharing it on social media?

    - A) Yes, I fact-check using credible sources. (3 points)

- B) Sometimes, but I mostly trust what I see. (2 points)

- C) No, I share things that look interesting without checking. (0 points)

Section 4: Safe Posting Habits

- Do you post real-time updates about your location?

  - A) No, I wait until I leave a place before posting. (3 points)

  - B) Sometimes, but only in safe environments. (2 points)

  - C) Yes, I frequently share my live location. (0 points)

- Do you tag friends and family in posts without their permission?

  - A) No, I always ask before tagging. (3 points)

  - B) Sometimes, if I think they won't mind. (2 points)

  - C) Yes, I tag people without asking. (0 points)

- Do you read the terms and conditions before signing up for a new social media platform?

  - A) Yes, I review them carefully. (3 points)

  - B) Sometimes, but I usually just skim through. (2 points)

  - C) No, I accept them without reading. (0 points)

Scoring & Results

Add up your points to determine your social media safety level.

30 – 36 points: Digital Security Pro

- You take online security seriously and follow best practices to protect yourself from cyber threats. Keep up the good work!

20 – 29 points: Cautious but Could Improve

- You are aware of online risks and take some precautions, but there's room for improvement. Consider tightening your security settings and habits.

10 – 19 points: At Risk

- You are vulnerable to cyber threats. Review your social media practices and take steps to enhance your online safety.

0 – 9 points: High Risk

- Your online habits expose you to significant risks. It's time to take social media security seriously—update your settings, enable 2FA, and be cautious with what you share online.

Conclusion

Being aware of your social media safety is the first step in protecting yourself online. Whether you scored high or low, there's always room to improve and strengthen your digital security habits. Stay vigilant, update your privacy settings, and continue learning about online safety.

Taking Control of Your Digital Safety

In an era where online spaces have become an integral part of daily life, ensuring digital safety is not just a precaution but a necessity. By equipping girls with the knowledge, tools, and confidence to navigate the digital world securely, we are fostering a generation that is empowered to take control of their online presence.

Key Takeaways

- **Knowledge is Power** – Understanding online risks, from cyber harassment to misinformation, allows girls to make informed decisions about their digital interactions.

- **Privacy Matters** – Practicing strong password habits, enabling two-factor authentication (2FA), and being mindful of sharing personal information online are crucial steps in safeguarding one's digital footprint.

- **Recognizing & Reporting Threats** – Knowing how to identify cyber threats, harassment, and scams, and taking immediate action by reporting and blocking offenders can prevent further harm.

- **Digital Detox & Mental Well-being** – Taking breaks from social media, setting healthy screen time limits, and prioritizing real-life connections contribute to a balanced and healthier digital lifestyle.

- **Support Networks** – No one should face online threats alone. Seeking help from trusted friends, family, or online safety organizations can provide the necessary support and guidance.

Moving Forward: A Call to Action

Empowering girls to stay safe online is an ongoing mission. Schools, parents, and digital platforms must play an active role in fostering awareness and implementing protective measures. Future advancements in cybersecurity, AI, and social media policies should prioritize user safety, ensuring that online spaces remain a place for positive engagement and growth.

Final Words

Online safety is not about fear—it's about empowerment. By staying informed, vigilant, and proactive, every girl can build her own **Digital Shield**—a strong defense against cyber threats while embracing the opportunities the digital world has to offer.

About the Author: Fazal Abubakkar Esaf

Fazal Abubakkar Esaf is a passionate advocate for digital security, online privacy, and responsible technology use. With a deep understanding of cybersecurity, social media ethics, and the evolving digital landscape, he has dedicated his work to educating individuals on how to navigate the online world safely.

Driven by a mission to empower people—especially young users—against cyber threats, Fazal combines extensive research with real-world insights to create practical guides that help readers stay informed and protected. His work delves into topics such as online harassment, misinformation, deepfake technology, and digital wellness, offering actionable strategies to counteract modern cyber risks.

Beyond writing, Fazal actively engages in awareness campaigns and discussions on digital safety, emphasizing the importance of cyber hygiene, ethical tech usage, and online responsibility. His work serves as a valuable resource for anyone looking to strengthen their digital defenses in an increasingly connected world.